Recipes For Busy People

W9-BFT-222

Contained here are the winning 300 entries out of the over 10,000 original recipes submitted by the busy people who work for Kelly Services throughout the U.S. and Canada.

As the best of the food critic's choices, these creative and compact recipes reflect varied lifestyles and needs —with the accent always on the preparation of tasty, nutritious, and satisfying meals.

Whether it's for quick, economical after-work dining, or for gracious hosting in leisure hours, here you'll learn how to plan, prepare, and enjoy:

- Appealing Appetizers
- Tasty and Satisfying Soups
- Mouthwatering Main Dish Entrees
- Savory Salads and Dressings
- Varied and Versatile Vegetables
- Dazzling Delectable Desserts
- Quick Breads, Cookies, Baked Goods
- Brown-Bag Specials
- Diet Dishes that Delight
- Bar-B-Q Bonanzas

With these "Recipes for Busy People" you'll never be too busy to enjoy the best in good food. *Bon Appetit from Kelly!*

RECIPES
for
BUSY
PEOPLE

How to prepare good and satisfying foods
after a day's work, cook up a party dish or
pack a "Brown Bag" lunch—the 300 best recipes
of busy people who work, chosen from
almost 10,000 submitted.

KELLY
SERVICES

The
"Kelly Girl"
People

Edited by Sylvia Schur

WARNER BOOKS

A Warner Communications Company

WARNER BOOKS EDITION

ISBN: 0-446-91542-4

Book design by Helen Roberts

Warner Books, Inc., 75 Rockefeller Plaza, New York, N.Y. 10019

A Warner Communications Company

Printed in the United States of America

First Printing: April, 1980

10 9 8 7 6 5 4 3

Contents

About Kelly Services, Inc.

Kelly people are experts at fitting into varied business situations . . . and these recipes are proof that they can apply the same flexibility and versatility to cooking ventures. The end result is "the true taste of success"—an outstanding collection of quick-to-fix recipes, new twists on family favorites, and some superb traditional dishes that please any palate. I'd like to thank the thousands of Kelly employees who took the time from their busy schedules to make this cookbook possible.

T.E. Adderley, President
Kelly Services, Inc.

About Vic Tayback

I never thought, when I was going to Acting School at night, and employed by Kelly Services during the day, that I'd end up enjoying the good dishes I tasted at the Busy People's Recipe Contest Cook-Off. They served my Chili! My cook's hat, which I wear on CBS-TV's "Alice," is off to these recipe winners. I'm proud to share the dishes of my fellow "Kelly Girls!"

Vic Tayback, TV Celebrity

About the Contest Recipes

All of us at Creative Food Service, Inc. enjoyed preparing and rating these fine, unique recipes. As professional cooks and testers we attempted to maintain the true characteristics and consistency of the recipes as indicated by each contestant.

Sylvia Schur, Editor

East-West Coast Winners Tie for Top Prizes

Excitement mounted in the Beverly Wilshire Hotel in Hollywood, California as Vic Tayback and a panel of Food Editor judges weighed the merits and flavors of the top 10 dishes. A detailed rating system was used which scored Appearance, Taste, Texture, Ease/Practicality and Creativity.

Finally, two recipes emerged as favorites. So close in score were they that the judges asked Kelly to authorize duplicate top awards to Elaine B. Poffenroth of Edmonds, Washington for her Wilted Lettuce Soup (see Soup chapter) and Pamela Bartlett of Stamford, Connecticut for her Apple Torte (see Baking chapter).

A Word About the Winners

Elaine B. Poffenroth returned to work via the secretarial route. She is active in her church and is the first woman to serve on its Officers' Council. She enjoys preparing traditional dishes, with farmstyle accents derived from her mother's German heritage. Ms. Poffenroth is married and her four grown children enjoy the family recipes.

Pamela Bartlett is a supervisor in Kelly Services Stamford, Connecticut branch office. Her husband Robert enjoyed taste-testing her recipes—and those of the other finalists at the cook-off.

RECIPES
FOR
BUSY
PEOPLE

Appetizers

Appetizers are important as a break between work and the rest of the meal . . . a selection of these could make a party. The winning appetizer, Gouda Deviled Tomatoes, is a baked dish you might also serve as a light lunch entree. Gary Edwin Kidd drummed this one up. This Kelly employee is not only a great cook but an accomplished musician too.

Annette Pugliese
Brooklyn, NY

Asparagus Fritters

Preparation time: 20 minutes

1 can (14 ounces)
asparagus tips or stems
and tips
1 egg, well beaten
½ cup milk
⅓ cup grated Italian
cheese
1 cup flavored Italian
bread crumbs for
mixture

Pinch salt and pepper
Pinch garlic powder
1 cup flavored bread
crumbs for coating
1 cup vegetable oil

Drain all liquid from can. Turn asparagus can onto a paper towel and let asparagus tips lie on the towel. Place a second towel on top and press down with your hand in order to blot as much liquid as possible from the asparagus. Discard paper towels. In a bowl mash asparagus with a fork, until consistency seems mushy. Add the egg and milk which have already been beaten together in a small cup. Next add the remaining ingredients except the oil, and crumbs for coating. Form this mixture in your palms into oval shaped fritters and roll slightly in a small amount of bread crumbs to coat the fritters. You should get about 10 to 12 fritters of about 2 to 3 inches in size. Fry in oil in a fry pan till golden on tops and then bottoms. Drain on paper towel. Serve immediately with cocktails. Yield: 10-12 fritters.

Judith Crothers
New Canaan, CT

Asparagus with Sour Cream Sauce

Preparation time: 20 minutes

2 pounds asparagus
½ cup sour cream
1 tablespoon horseradish, drained

½ teaspoon lemon juice
Pinch salt and white pepper

Wash asparagus, snap off tough ends and trim stalks. With a vegetable peeler strip them a few inches below tips to remove scales. Stand stalks in bottom of a double boiler half full of boiling, salted water and cover with the inverted top of the double boiler. Cook over high heat for about 10 minutes, or until stalks are just tender. Drain and put on platter to cool. Arrange cold asparagus on serving plates. Mix together sour cream, horseradish, lemon juice, salt and pepper. Spoon over asparagus. Makes 4 servings.

Rebecca A. Harris
Eugene, OR

Cashew-Stuffed Mushrooms

Preparation time: 30 minutes

¼–½ pound of raw cashews, chopped (Health food stores have them in bulk.)

4 green onions, chopped

1 cup bread crumbs (whole wheat is easier to crumb and tastes good)

¼ cup melted butter

½ teaspoon oregano

25–30 of the largest mushrooms you can find; try to get the freshest. They will be whiter and not opened at the bottom, so "gills" will not show.

Additional butter

Sour cream

Sliced olives

Preheat the oven to 350°. Mix the cashews, chopped green onions, bread crumbs, melted butter and oregano together in a bowl. Wipe off mushrooms with a damp cloth. Be careful not to get them wet, as they get soggy. Twist off stems, being careful to retain bowl-like shape of caps. Butter outsides of caps. Fill each cap to overflowing with mixture. Place a small dab of butter on each cap. Put caps on an oiled cookie sheet with a little space between each one. Cook for 10 minutes. Garnish with sour cream and olive slice. Serves 4 to 8.

Ann Wyman
Montclair, CA

Cheese Ball

Preparation time: 10 minutes, plus chilling time

- 2 packages (8 ounces each) cream cheese
- ½ cup crumbled blue cheese (optional)
- 1 cup soft butter
- 1 tablespoon caraway seed
- 1 tablespoon chopped pimiento
- 1 tablespoon chopped onion
- 1 tablespoon Worcestershire sauce
- ½ teaspoon paprika
- ½ teaspoon salt
- Dash of pepper
- Chopped pecans

Cream cheese and butter. Add remaining ingredients, except pecans. Form into a ball. Place in refrigerator several hours. Roll ball in finely chopped pecans. Serve with crackers. Makes 10-12 servings.

Judith L. Topletz
Richardson, TX

Chichikopista
(German Cocktail Meatballs with Sauerkraut)

Preparation time: 40 minutes

1 pound ground veal or
beef
4 teaspoons chopped
parsley
1 clove garlic, minced
⅔ cup fine rye bread
crumbs
½ medium onion, finely
diced
1 egg
2 teaspoons paprika

1 teaspoon salt
¼ teaspoon freshly ground
black pepper
1 tablespoon caraway seed
1 can or jar (1 pound)
Bavarian style
sauerkraut
½ cup Riesling wine (or
other white wine)
Dijon or Hot Chinese
mustard (optional)

In a large bowl, mix the first ten ingredients by hand until completely blended. Form the mixture into cocktail-sized balls. Brown the meatballs in an electric skillet on medium heat or in a skillet over medium flame. After all the meatballs have been browned, drain excess fat and cover them with the sauerkraut, then pour wine over all. Simmer, covered, 15-20 minutes. Serve in a chafing dish with mustard as accompaniment. Makes 4-6 servings. This dish can also be used as the entree for a light supper.

Marty Hayworth
Colorado Springs, CO

Chinese Egg Rolls with Sweet and Sour Sauce

Preparation time: 30 minutes

- ¼ cup chopped onion
- 1 pound pork or chicken (cut into small pieces or ground)
- 1 small cabbage
- 1 celery stalk and leaf
- 1 carrot
- 1 green onion
- Soy sauce, salt and pepper (to taste)
- 1 package egg roll skins
- Vegetable oil for frying

Brown chopped onion and meat until tender. Shred cabbage, celery, carrot, and green onion. Brown together with meat, add soy sauce, salt and pepper. Be sure it doesn't get mushy. Drain any juices. Fold in eggroll skin; secure edges with water. Fry quickly in hot oil till brown and outside is crunchy. Makes 10-15 large egg rolls. Serve with Sweet and Sour Sauce (below). May substitute Won Ton skins—great for parties!

Sweet and Sour Sauce:

- 1 can (1 pound, 4 ounces) pineapple chunks
- 1 cup sugar
- 2 tablespoons cornstarch
- ¾ cup cider vinegar
- 1 tablespoon soy sauce
- ¼ teaspoon ginger
- 1 chicken bouillon cube

Drain pineapple. Add enough water to juice to measure 1¼ cups. In medium saucepan, combine all ingredients and bring to boil. Boil for 2 minutes. Serve.

A. Samantha Polfelt
Philadelphia, PA

Clams 'a la Sam

Preparation time: 15 minutes

1 dozen clams (in shell)	½ cup water
1 bunch scallions	½ stick butter (optional
1 clove garlic	if dieting)
1 cup white wine	

Wash clams well. Chop scallions, crush garlic, and add with wine and water to large pot. Put clams on top. Put lid on pot and steam till clams open, about 5 minutes. Add melted butter to clam broth for extra flavor. Serve with French bread and finish off the wine! Serves 2.

Billie R. Locke
Nashville, TN

Crab Balls

Preparation time: 50 minutes

2 teaspoons margarine	⅛ teaspoon black pepper
4 teaspoons flour	½ cup cornstarch
⅓ cup sweet milk	3½ cups vegetable oil—
1 can (6 ounces) drained	heated to 375° for deep-
crabmeat	fat frying of crab balls
¼ teaspoon salt	

Melt margarine in small pan. Gradually add flour and stir until smooth. Add milk and stir until the mixture begins to boil and take on a sauce-like appearance. Stir in crabmeat, salt and pepper. Refrigerate and chill for 25-30 minutes. After chilling, form the crab mixture into approximately 25 teaspoon-size balls. Roll them in cornstarch. Drop into preheated deep-fat frying pan of oil and cook about 3 minutes. Remove with slotted spoon and drain on paper towel. Serve hot with horseradish or soy sauce. Makes 4 servings.

Susan Watkins
Atlanta, GA

Creamy Bacon Dip

Preparation time: 20 minutes

4 slices very lean bacon, diced
¼ cup onion, diced
½ medium bell pepper, diced
½ teaspoon salt
½ teaspoon minced garlic
¼ teaspoon cracked pepper

1 tablespoon flour
3 ounces cream cheese at room temperature
⅓ cup sour cream
1 teaspoon soy sauce
1 teaspoon Worcestershire sauce

Saute bacon until crunchy. Remove bacon and leave 2 tablespoons drippings. Saute onion and bell pepper until soft. Add salt, garlic, cracked pepper and flour, saute 1-2 minutes longer, remove from heat. In a serving bowl, mix cream cheese and sour cream. Mix in soy sauce and Worcestershire sauce. Stir in the bacon and onion mixture. Serve with garlic flavored crackers and melba toast. Makes approximately 2 servings. (This "dip" can also be used in omelets, on baked potatoes, to top broiled steaks or English muffins. Also, thinned with beef stock, this makes an excellent soup.)

Dr. Sherry Rice Blanchard
Dallas, TX

Dolmas

Preparation time: 1½ hours, plus chilling time

1 jar (16 ounces) grape
  leaves in brine
1 pound ground lamb
1 pound ground veal
1 egg, beaten
2 onions, chopped
2 garlic cloves, chopped
½ cup chopped parsley
1 teaspoon salt

1 tablespoon pepper
2 cups cooked rice (al
  dente)
2 lemons, sliced thin
2 cups yogurt, plain or
  homemade
½ cup chopped mint
2 packages pita bread

Fill your sink with ice water and rinse grape leaves well. Mix ground meats, egg, onion, garlic, parsley, spices and cooked rice. Separate grape leaves. Lay 1 flat on your chopping block. Fill with approximately 1 heaping tea-spoon mixture. Fold point of leaf over, then each side and roll. Do this until all the leaves are used. Arrange on plate, cover and refrigerate 1 hour or until chilled. Take steamer or large pot and add about ¼ inch water on bottom. Gently arrange stuffed leaves in pot. Slice one of the lemons very thinly and arrange slices all over leaves. Cover and steam very slowly one hour. Serve hot with fresh sliced lemon, yogurt (sprinkled with mint if you like) and warmed pita bread. It is traditional to tear the pita bread into pieces, place the Dolma on the pita bread and dip in the yogurt. Can be kept in the refrigerator but does not freeze well. Makes 10-15 servings.

Pamela Jayne Locke
Ghent, KY

Ever Ready Cheese Log

Preparation time: 15 minutes, plus chilling time

- ½ pound sharp cheese, grated
- 1½ tablespoons minced onion
- 3 tablespoons chopped green pepper
- 3 chopped stuffed olives
- 2 tablespoons minced pickle
- 1 tablespoon minced pimiento
- 1 hard boiled egg, minced
- ½ cup crushed soda crackers
- ½ cup mayonnaise
- ½ teaspoon salt

Combine all ingredients and form into a long roll. Wrap in wax paper and refrigerate until firm. Serve sliced, with crackers. Makes 4-6 servings.

Karen F. Kile
Springfield, OR

"Georgia's" Bean Dip

Preparation time: 1 hour

- 1 can (1 pound) refried beans
- 1 pound ground beef Salt, pepper, garlic powder, chili powder to taste
- 1 small can chopped chili peppers
- ¼ pound fresh chopped mushrooms
- 1 cup taco sauce
- ½ cup each grated Monterey Jack and Cheddar cheese
- 1 small can chopped black olives
- 4-6 green onions, sliced
- 1 medium avocado, mashed
- ½ cup sour cream

Spread refried beans on the bottom of a slightly oiled casserole dish (3-4 quart size). Brown the ground beef in a frying pan and season with salt, pepper, garlic, chili powder, etc. Spread the meat over the beans and sprinkle the chopped chili peppers and chopped fresh mushrooms over the meat. Drizzle a cup of taco over the mixture and then pile mounds of grated Monterey Jack and Cheddar cheese over the top. Sprinkle with chopped black olives and green onions. Bake at 350° for 45 minutes. Serve hot, garnished with mashed avocado and sour cream. Serve with corn chips and taco chips. Makes 4-6 servings. Note: Diced white meat of chicken can be used instead of the ground meat for a different taste.

Gary E. Kidd
Bloomfield Hills, MI

Gouda Deviled Tomatoes

Preparation time: Approx. 60 minutes

2 *large tomatoes*
Salt, pepper
1 *hard cooked egg*
¼ *cup softened unsalted sweet butter*
½ *cup grated Gouda cheese*

⅓ *cup chopped boiled ham*
2 *egg yolks*
2 *egg whites*
Watercress

Preheat oven to 375°. Prepare tomatoes: Remove ½ inch slice from tops of tomatoes. Scoop out pulp and reserve for another use. Sprinkle insides of tomatoes with salt and pepper, invert and drain on paper toweling.

Prepare filling: Remove yolk from hard cooked egg and mash with butter in a medium size bowl. Chop hard cooked egg white and stir together with cheese, ham and 2 egg yolks into butter mixture. Season to taste with salt

(22)

and pepper. Beat 2 egg whites in small bowl till stiff peaks form, then fold into cheese mixture.

Final preparation: Fill tomato cups with cheese mixture. Bake in oven for about 25 minutes. Garnish with watercress. Serves 2. Note: To serve 6, use 6 small tomatoes.

Elaine Wallace
Utica, NY

Ham, Cheese, Pepperoni Loaf

Preparation time: 50 to 60 minutes

11 eggs	*½ teaspoon salt*
¾ cup milk	*8 ounces Cheddar cheese*
1½ cups flour	*8 ounces Muenster cheese*
2½ teaspoons baking powder	*8 ounces ham*
	8 ounces pepperoni

Beat first 5 ingredients together. Then cut next 4 ingredients into small pieces and add to egg mixture. Pour into greased and flowered 13x9x2-inch pan. Bake at 350° for 50-60 minutes or until knife comes out clean and top is a golden color. Serve cold in small slices. Can be cut in 3 individual loaves; freezes nicely for future use. Makes 16 servings.

Angela Payne
Longmeadow, MA

Herb Dip

Preparation time: 10 minutes

½ cup sour cream
½ cup mayonnaise
2 tablespoons of fresh
 parsley, chopped
2 tablespoons chives
2 tablespoons chopped
 onions

1 clove garlic, minced
1 teaspoon Worcestershire
 sauce
 Dash Tabasco sauce,
 salt and pepper
1 cup cottage cheese,
 pureed in blender

Mix everything except cottage cheese, then mix the two together. Since this is a dip, you will need something to dip. I recommend that you use fresh vegetables. You should use things like tomatoes, celery sticks, cucumber sticks, carrot sticks and other fresh vegetables. Place the dip in the refrigerator to chill then serve with the fresh vegetables surrounding the dip. Makes 6-8 servings.

Jeannean Thompson
Borger, TX

Honey Chicken Wings

Preparation time: 1 hour or longer

3 pounds chicken wings
 Salt and pepper
1 cup honey
½ cup soy sauce

2 tablespoons vegetable
 oil
2 tablespoons catsup
½ garlic clove, chopped

Cut off and discard chicken wing tips. Cut each wing into two parts and sprinkle with salt and pepper. Combine remaining ingredients and mix well. Place wings in slow cooker and pour sauce over. Cook all day on low setting. Or, preheat oven to 375°. Place wings in shallow casserole, pour sauce over and bake 1 hour, until chicken is well done and sauce is caramelized. Serves approximately 10.

Sandra Mortimore
Walnut Creek, CA

Italian Fritta

Preparation time: 30 minutes

4 medium zucchini
¼ cup or little more vegetable oil
1 medium white onion
6–8 eggs
1 cup grated Parmesan cheese (save ¼ cup for top)
2 teaspoons dried or fresh chopped parsley
1 teaspoon basil

¼ teaspoon oregano
⅛ teaspoon marjoram
⅛ teaspoon thyme
1 teaspoon garlic powder
Salt and pepper
1 small jar of sliced mushrooms, drained (optional)
¼ teaspoon cream of tartar
2 tablespoons butter or margarine

Cut the zucchini in half lengthwise, blanch in boiling salted water for a few minutes, and drain. Cut into ¼ inch slices. Cover bottom of 8-inch iron skillet with oil. Chop or slice onion and saute in oil till slightly brown. In large bowl break eggs. Add Parmesan cheese (save ¼ cup for top). Beat. Add herbs, zucchini, mushrooms, cream of tartar, garlic powder, salt and pepper. Beat well. When onions are nicely limp add about 2 tablespoons of butter or margarine, then add egg mixture and mix well with onions. Place in 350° oven for about 25 minutes until light brown. Let cool. Scoop knife around edges and under with spatula. Turn over onto serving platter. May be eaten when cool or refrigerate for next day. Serves 6 to 8.

(25)

Jeanette Kral
Omaha, NE

Kelly Kooler

Preparation time: 15 minutes, plus freezing time

2 cups sugar
9 cups water
12 ounces frozen orange
  juice concentrate
12 ounces frozen lemonade
  concentrate

4 green tea bags
2½ cups rum or vodka
Lemon-lime soda or
  lemon-sour soda

Mix together 2 cups sugar, 7 cups water, orange concentrate and lemon concentrate in large saucepan. Bring to a boil and then cool. Add the 4 green tea bags to 2 cups boiling water and let steep for a few minutes. Squeeze all of the water out of the tea bags and add the water to the first mixture. Stir well and add the rum or vodka. Put the mixture into a plastic container, cover and freeze. The mixture will not freeze solid due to the rum or vodka. When ready to serve, spoon into a 6-ounce glass until 2/3 full, add soda and stir well. Garnish with a lemon, lime, orange or cherry and have a Kelly Kooler. Makes approximately 30 servings.

Sally Hoene
W. St. Paul, MN

Lagougere (Souffle)

Preparation time: 45 minutes

¾ cup water
¼ cup butter
  Pinch salt, pepper
½ cup flour

3 eggs
¾ cup Swiss cheese,
  grated with a potato
  peeler

Heat to boiling the water, butter and salt. Remove immediately from the heat. Add the flour and stir quickly with a wooden spoon until well mixed. Put pan back on reduced heat and stir dough often for 2 or 3 minutes. Take it off the heat again and stir in 1 egg at a time—thoroughly and quickly. When all the eggs are added, stir in first the pepper, then ½ cup of the Swiss cheese. Place the batter in a ring on a greased pan in the form of a "crown." Place extra cheese around the top. Bake at 375° for 30 minutes. It should rise like a souffle, so serve it immediately before it falls—it looks nicer.

Claire Stolzer
Philadelphia, PA

Liverwurst "Igloo"

Preparation time: 25 minutes

½ pound chunk liverwurst	2 tablespoons milk
1 teaspoon chopped onion	½ teaspoon Tabasco sauce
½ teaspoon basil	Dash garlic salt
Dash garlic salt	
3 ounces cream cheese (softened)	

Mix first 4 ingredients in bowl; form into "igloo" shape and refrigerate at least 1 hour. Mix cream cheese with milk, add Tabasco sauce and garlic salt and spread over liverwurst. Serve on wafer thin crackers or small sliced party rye. Makes 2-4 servings.

Johnell Lambe
Fresno, CA

Marinated Mushrooms

Preparation time: 45 minutes, plus chilling time

1 cup vinegar
2 cups water
½ teaspoon salt
1 teaspoon pepper
1½ pounds fresh mushrooms
¼ cup olive oil

½ teaspoon oregano
½ teaspoon crushed red pepper
¼ cup chopped parsley
½ teaspoon garlic powder
4 sweet basil leaves

Bring vinegar, water, salt and ½ teaspoon pepper to a rolling boil. Add mushrooms; cook 5 minutes. Drain and let stand 30 minutes. Combine olive oil, ½ teaspoon pepper, oregano, crushed red pepper, parsley, garlic powder and basil. Add mushrooms and refrigerate 24 hours. Salt to taste. Makes 6 servings.

Sylvia Rossman
East Windsor, NJ

Mozzy Mushy Clam Dip

Preparation time: 40 minutes

½ medium onion, diced
2 tablespoons salad oil
¼ cup bread crumbs
1 can (2 ounces) chopped mushrooms, drained
½ teaspoon ground oregano
1 teaspoon dehydrated parsley flakes

½ teaspon garlic powder
1 can (8 ounces) minced clams with liquid
4 ounces diced mozzarella cheese
Extra bread crumbs, Parmesan cheese and garlic powder for topping

(28)

Saute onion in oil 3 minutes, add next 5 ingredients and saute 1 minute more. Remove from heat and add clams and liquid. Grease a 1½ quart casserole dish and alternate layers of clam mixture and diced mozzarella cheese. Top with mixture of ¼ cup grated Parmesan cheese, ¼ cup bread crumbs and ½ teaspoon garlic powder. Bake in 350° oven for 30 minutes or until mozzarella cheese is bubbling. Serve hot with crackers. Makes 2 servings, or a snack for 4 people.

Mary L. Hardesty
Chula Vista, CA

Mushroom Roll-Ups

Preparation time: 60 minutes

1 pound frozen bread
  dough
½ pound fresh mushrooms,
  sliced
4 slices bacon
2 cups Cheddar cheese,
  shredded

1 egg, beaten
2 tablespoons minced
  onion
4 tablespoons melted
  margarine

Let dough thaw to room temperature. Roll out on a lightly floured surface to form a rectangle, 12x16 inches. Clean mushrooms and thinly slice. Fry bacon until crisp. Drain bacon strips on paper towel. Use bacon drippings to saute the mushrooms for 5 minutes, stirring frequently. Drain off as much of the bacon grease as possible. Combine mushrooms, cheese, egg, onion, and crumbled bacon then spread this mixture on top of dough leaving a 1-inch margin clean all around. Roll up dough, jelly-roll fashion, making a tight roll. Cut into 1-inch slices. Use ½ of the melted margarine to grease a 7x11-inch oblong pan, or you can use two 8-inch layer cake pans, and arrange the roll-ups cut side down side by side. Cover with a tea towel and allow dough to rise triple in volume. Dribble remaining margarine over tops. Bake at 375° for 25-30 minutes, or until roll-ups are a golden brown. Turn out at once. Serve warm or cold. Makes about 16 rolls.

Scott Buchanan
San Jose, CA

Outtasite Avocado Dip

Preparation time: 10 minutes

1 large or 2 small
   avocados, ripe
8 ounces real sour cream
3 generous tablespoons
   mayonnaise

½ teaspoon lemon juice
1 teaspoon onion flakes, or
   sprinkle onion salt

Peel and pit avocados. Mash them into an even creamy paste with a fork. Add remaining ingredients and mix well. If you use onion flakes, let dip set for at least 20 minutes. Serves 2 as snack for whole evening or buys your way into a party.

Variation 1: Add 1½ teaspoons chili powder, several drops hot sauce and ½ chopped tomato (or 2 tablespoons spaghetti sauce swiped from a jar of Ragu).

Variation 2: Take 6 corn tortillas (left over from yesterday's tacos?) and cut into triangular sixths. Put ½ inch of oil in a frying pan and add tortilla pieces when oil just begins to smoke. Be sure to flip the chips. When cooked crisp, drain on paper towels. Salt these chips while they are hot and draining. Use for dipping.

Judith Dubrinsky
Troy, MI

Pickled Shrimp

Preparation time: 40 minutes

1 pound fresh or frozen
shrimp in the shells
¼ cup celery tops
2 tablespoons mixed
pickling spices

1 tablespoon salt
1 cup sliced onions
4 or 5 bay leaves

Pickling Marinade:

¾ cup cooking oil
⅓ cup white vinegar
2 tablespoons capers and
juice
1 teaspoon celery seed

½ teaspoon salt
1 drop Tabasco sauce
1 drop Worcestershire
sauce

Cover shrimp with boiling water; add celery tops, pickling spices, and salt. Cover and simmer for 5 minutes. Drain, then peel and devein under cold water. Alternate cleaned shrimp, onions and bay leaves in shallow baking dish. Combine remaining ingredients for Pickling Marinade. Mix well. Pour over shrimp. Cover; chill at least 24 hours, spooning marinade over shrimp occasionally. Drain, remove bay leaves. Serve shrimp and onion slices on a relish tray. (Pickled Shrimp will keep at least a week in refrigerator.) The beauty of this recipe is that you can prepare it ahead of time and when you are ready the shrimp is ready. It is also a great recipe for a picnic by putting the shrimp in a covered glass or plastic container and placing in your picnic basket. Makes 2 generous servings.

Pat Soden
Walnut Creek, CA

Quick Chili Con Queso

Preparation time: 15 minutes

1 medium onion, chopped
1 clove garlic, crushed
2 tablespoons butter or margarine
1 large tomato, finely chopped
½ cup chopped green chilies
½ teaspoon oregano
¼ teaspoon salt
1 pound Cheddar cheese, cut in cubes
Corn chips or potato chips

Lightly brown onion and garlic in butter. Add all other ingredients except cheese and chips. You can use a saucepan over very low heat, but an electric fondue pot set on "cheese" can be used and then the chili can be served in it also. Stir in cheese until it melts. Serve with corn chips or potato chips. Makes 10 servings.

Shirley Trackwell
Taylor, MI

Salmon-blue Cheese Appetizer

Preparation time: 20-25 minutes

1 can (1 pound) salmon, boned, flaked and drained
2 ounces blue cheese
8 ounces cream cheese
1 tablespoon grated onion
1 tablespoon lemon juice
2 dashes Tabasco sauce

Combine all ingredients into a paste-like mixture. Shape into a ball or a fish (use olives for eyes). Chill, decorate with parsley, lemon slices. Serve with crackers. Makes 6 servings.

Gladys Dunsker
Somerville, NJ

Sardine Savory

Preparation time: 20 minutes

2 slices firm white bread
½ can Portuguese skinless and boneless sardines in oil
1 teaspoon lemon juice
1 tablespoon mayonnaise
½ small thinly sliced tomato

2 slices packaged American cheese
2 slices bacon—each slice cut in thirds and half cooked

Toast bread lightly in toaster and set aside. Mash drained sardines with lemon juice and mayonnaise. Spread half on each slice of toast, spreading evenly to the very edges. Cover with thin slices of tomato and cut each open sandwich into 3 strips. Cut each slice of cheese into thirds and place one piece of cheese on each strip of sandwich. Top each with 1 small piece (third of a slice) of half cooked bacon and place appetizers on broiler pan lined with aluminum foil. Place about 6 inches from flame in oven broiler and broil until cheese is evenly browned and bacon is crisp. Serve at once. This takes about 10 minutes. It should be broiled slowly in order to heat through thoroughly. Serves 2 with a cocktail or tomato juice. Recipe can be doubled or increased by any amount to serve more people. It can also be prepared completely early in the day and placed on broiler pan and covered with plastic wrap and refrigerated until just before serving and then broiled. In this case, allow about 5 minutes more to ensure that the sandwiches are heated through. Serve at once.

Liz Owen
Sunnymead, CA

Shrimp Avocado Cocktail

Preparation time: 45 minutes

- 1 package (3 ounces) cream cheese, softened
- 2 tablespoons chili sauce
- 1 tablespoon lemon juice
- 1 teaspoon grated onion
- 1 teaspoon Worcestershire sauce
- ¼ teaspoon salt
- 1 large avocado, seeded, peeled and cubed
- 8 ounces cooked shrimp, shelled, deveined and chilled
- ½ cup celery
- Lettuce cups

In small bowl, combine cream cheese, chili sauce, lemon juice, onion, Worcestershire and salt. Blend until smooth. Chill thoroughly. Combine avocado, shrimp and celery; divide among 4 lettuce-lined sherbets. Top with sauce. Makes 4 servings.

Catherine H. Fee
Whitesboro, NY

Shrimp Mousse

Preparation time: 35 minutes, plus chilling time

- 1 envelope unflavored gelatin
- ¼ cup cold water
- 1 can tomato soup, undiluted
- 1 package (8 ounces) cream cheese
- 1 cup mayonnaise
- 1 can (4½ ounces) small shrimp, rinsed and drained
- ½ cup each finely chopped onion, celery, green pepper
- 2 slices pimiento stuffed olive

Dissolve gelatin in water. Set aside. Heat soup in saucepan. Keep boiling and mix in the cream cheese with beater. Remove from heat and stir in gelatin. Cool a few minutes and add mayonnaise, shrimp and vegetables. Mix thoroughly and pour into slightly oiled fish mold. Unmold on serving tray. Place a slice of green olive with pimiento for eye of fish. Serve with assorted crackers. This is best if made a day ahead of time. A great crowd pleaser. Makes 12 servings.

Kathy Beall
Norcross, GA

Spanish Tortilla

Preparation time: 30 minutes

½ pound bacon
¼ cup olive oil (don't substitute)
¼ cup finely chopped green pepper
¼ cup finely chopped onion

4 medium potatoes, diced
3 cloves garlic
2 medium eggs
½ teaspoon salt
½ teaspoon freshly ground black pepper

Fry bacon until crisp and set aside to drain. Heat olive oil in large pan. Chop pepper, onion, potatoes and garlic and add to hot oil. Cook over medium heat until almost brown and remove and drain. With remaining olive oil, heat in 8-inch straight sided pan (to give pie shape). Mix eggs, salt and pepper, then add crumbled bacon to mixture along with vegetables. Mix well. In hot oil pour in mixture and press firmly to shape to pan and cook over low heat long enough to brown egg, about 8 minutes. Turn using a plate over the pan and brown egg on other side. Serve hot and slice like a pie. Makes 2-4 servings.

K.L. Boles
Columbus, OH

Spicy Eggplant Tostadas

Preparation time: 20 minutes

½ of a small eggplant, cut
   into slices about ⅓ inch
   thick
Salt
Whole wheat flour for
   coating eggplant slices
Oil (olive or corn)
Pinto or kidney beans, 1
   single serving size can
Taco sauce (tomato-
   based variety with
   minced vegetables)

½ cup grated sharp
   Cheddar cheese
⅓ medium sized green bell
   pepper, chopped fine
About 5 pitted black
   olives, sliced for
   garnish

Wash and slice eggplant; sprinkle slices with salt and let
set. Pour about ⅓ cup flour into cereal bowl. Then pour
approximately ⅛ inch oil into medium-sized heavy skillet and begin heating over a medium-high heat setting.
Heat beans over a low fire in a covered saucepan. Rinse
salt from eggplant and pat slices dry; coat with flour.
When oil is hot enough to fry quickly a bit of bread crust,
place slices in skillet. Fry them approximately one minute;
turn them and fry until tender. Transfer slices to paper-
towel covered plate and blot away excess oil. Cover each
slice thinly with taco sauce, then with the heated beans;
sprinkle with grated cheese. Garnish with green peppers
and a few olive slices, and serve at once (or keep for a
few minutes in oven). Makes 2 servings. Note: This filling
appetizer is good served before a light dinner of gazpacho,
chilled and heavily laced with lime juice (fresh only)
and diced jicama. Plain tortilla chips and mild guacamole
should be served on the side.

Nancy Ofiara
Melbourne, FL

Stuffed Mushrooms

Preparation time: 45 minutes

½ cup (1 stick) butter
24 mushrooms, 1 to 1½ inches in diameter
½ teaspoon crushed garlic
1 tablespoon finely chopped parsley
½ cup coarsely chopped pecans

¼ cup plus 1 tablespoon cream sherry
⅛ teaspoon salt
1½ cups fresh bread crumbs
2 tablespoons coarsely grated Jarlsberg (or any Swiss) cheese

Melt butter in large skillet. Remove and chop mushroom stems. Saute mushroom caps over medium heat, 5 minutes each side. Remove mushroom caps from pan and place on oven-proof serving platter. To same skillet, add mushroom stems and saute until they just begin to brown, about 7-10 minutes. Add garlic, parsley and pecans. Stir 1 minute. Add ¼ cup sherry, simmer until sherry has evaporated. Add salt and bread crumbs, stir for 5 minutes. Remove from heat and sprinkle with 1 tablespoon sherry; toss lightly. Firmly pack each mushroom cap with bread crumb mixture, mounding slightly. Sprinkle each mushroom with cheese. Preheat oven to 400°. Bake for 7 minutes; serve immediately. Makes 24 stuffed mushrooms. May be prepared 3-4 days in advance and refrigerated. Preheat oven to 350°. Bake for 15 minutes. Makes 6 servings.

Judy Wittu
Arlington, TX

Tuna Balls in Tartar Sauce

Preparation time: 45 minutes

1 can (6½ ounces) tuna,
  drained
1 egg
½ cup cornmeal
¼ cup finely chopped
  onion

Pepper to taste
Water, enough to make
  mixture form a ball

Mix all ingredients in a bowl. Form into small balls and drop into hot fat (400°) until browned. Serve with tartar sauce. Makes 4 servings.

Tartar Sauce:

2 large kosher dill pickles
¼ cup onion
1 cup mayonnaise

1 tablespoon mustard
2 teaspoons parsley flakes

Chop pickles and onions very fine and add remaining ingredients. Chill.

Verna Kuczynski
South Bend, IN

Tuna Pate

Preparation time: 5 minutes

1 can (6½ ounces) flaked
  tuna in oil
¼ pound margarine
8 ounces cream cheese

½ teaspoon tarragon
1 small onion
1 tablespoon lemon juice
Chives

Drain tuna and blend all ingredients except chives in blender or food processor. Turn out into dish and top with chopped chives. Serve with crackers or rye bread. Makes about 2 cups.

Ava S. Fenko
Brooklyn, NY

Yapraki

Preparation time: Up to 2 hours

1 cup raw rice	1 cup tomato sauce
1 egg	1 head cabbage
1 pound ground beef	2 tablespoons oil
1 tablespoon wheat germ	2 tablespoons tomato paste
Salt, pepper	½ cup water or wine
Dash cloves	Pinch of basil
2 chopped onions	1 tablespoon lemon juice

Cook rice as usual, according to package directions. Mix cooked rice, egg, beef, wheat germ, salt, pepper, cloves, 1 onion, 2 tablespoons of the tomato sauce. Steam cabbage in a large kettle; remove leaves as they soften, until you have about 12 large, whole leaves. Reserve remaining cabbage for another use. Roll meat mixture into balls and wrap meat in cabbage leaves. Meanwhile, saute remaining onion in oil. Add tomato paste and water or wine, leftover tomato sauce, salt, pepper, basil and lemon juice. Allow to boil and add cabbage rolls. Simmer ¾ to one hour. Makes 6 servings.

Soups

Hot soups, cold soups, thick soups, smooth soups, chunky soups—soups are a savory way for busy people to round out a meal. Wilted Lettuce Soup, prize-winner in this category and a *grand prize winner*, is a favorite of Elaine Poffenroth of Edmonds, Washington, who joined Kelly Services in 1977 as a temporary secretary. She inherited her mother's talents in the kitchen . . . and hopes her four grown children will carry on the tradition.

Judy McLain
Fullerton, CA

Broccoli Soup

Preparation time: 30 minutes

Bunch of broccoli
1½ cups boiling water
2 cans (10½ ounces each)
cream of chicken soup

1 cup light cream
Salt, pepper, cayenne
Garnish: croutons

Wash and chop broccoli, boil in 1½ cups boiling water until tender. Using all liquid, put in blender and chop. Add remaining ingredients and heat. Season to taste with salt, pepper and cayenne. Top with croutons. Yields 5 cups.

Carolyn Bernfeld
New Rochelle, NY

Cantaloupe Soup

Preparation time: 5 minutes, plus chilling time

½ ripe cantaloupe
2 cups orange juice
1 tablespoon lime juice

¼ teaspoon cinnamon
Fresh mint sprigs

In a blender, blend diced pulp from cantaloupe with orange juice, lime juice, and cinnamon. Chill. Serve with mint garnish. Serves 2. Yield: 3½ cups.

John Benjamin Marion
Los Angeles, CA

Chicken and Mushroom Soup

Preparation time: 40 minutes

3 tablespoons butter or margarine

¼ cup finely chopped onion

1 pound mushrooms (sliced)

⅓ cup flour

4 cups chicken broth (canned broth can be used)

1½ cups half and half (or cream)

½ cup dry white wine (no specific brand needed)

1 teaspoon salt

½ teaspoon hot pepper sauce

2½ cups diced cooked chicken

¼ teaspoon tarragon
Chopped parsley for garnish

In a large pot or kettle melt butter over medium heat. Add onion and cook until tender. Add mushrooms and cook for 10 minutes. Next step, blend in flour and cook 1 minute. Stir in chicken broth and wine. Stir over medium heat until mixture thickens and comes to a boil. Add salt, hot pepper sauce, chicken and tarragon. Simmer uncovered for 20 minutes. Add half and half and heat. Garnish with parsley. Makes 4 to 6 servings.

Peggy Treleaven
Encino, CA

Cucumber Soup

Preparation time: 15 minutes, plus chilling time

*1 cup peeled, diced
    cucumber with tough
    seeds removed*
2 cups buttermilk
*1 tablespoon chives or
    green onion tips*

1 teaspoon soy sauce
½ teaspoon dill weed
2 teaspoons lemon juice

Combine all ingredients in blender until smooth. Chill until icy and serve in chilled bouillon cups. Garnish with thin slices of lemon or very coarse ground black pepper.

Dorothy R. Burleigh
Houston, TX

Curried Chicken Soup

Preparation time: 15 minutes

*½ cup cooked chicken, cut
    in small pieces*
2 teaspoons curry powder
½ teaspoon butter
*1 can (10½ ounces) cream
    of chicken soup*
1 cup half and half

*4 tablespoons lemon juice,
    or to taste*
*1 teaspoon fresh parsley;
    chopped*
2 lemon slices
2 tablespoons sour cream

Saute chicken, curry powder and butter in pan until warm and butter is melted. Slowly blend in can of condensed soup. Add 1 cup half and half. Heat but do not boil. Add lemon juice and parsley. Pour into soup bowls. Garnish with floating lemon slice topped with 1 tablespoon sour cream. Makes 2 servings.

Mary A. Kivisto
Ypsilanti, MI

Easy Summer Ragout

Preparation time: 30 minutes

1 small can (4 ounces)
    mushrooms

½ cup red wine or vinegar
    Pinch thyme, rosemary,
        salt and pepper

½ teaspoon garlic powder

1 small can (4 ounces)
    mushroom gravy

1 tablespoon butter

4 ounces sirloin steak,
    chopped fine

1 small onion, diced

1 small zucchini, peeled
    and diced

¼ cup eggplant, peeled,
    diced and salted

¼ cup diced celery

½ green pepper, diced

1 tomato, peeled and
    diced

6 water chestnuts, diced

¼ cup water

¼ cup cold strong coffee

Drain and reserve the liquid from the can of mushrooms; set mushrooms aside. In a saucepan mix together red wine, mushroom liquid, thyme, rosemary, garlic powder, salt and pepper. Allow to come to a boil. Add can of mushroom gravy; cook over low heat (approximately 5 minutes) until well blended. In a skillet melt butter. Add steak and onion. Saute meat and onion until tender (5-10 minutes). Remove from pan. Add zucchini and eggplant; saute until tender (5 minutes). Remove from pan. Add celery and green pepper; allow to cook 2-3 minutes until just crisp/tender. Return meat, onion, zucchini and eggplant to skillet and add mushrooms, tomato, and water chestnuts. Reduce heat. Allow to simmer for 5 minutes. Add vegetable/meat mixture to saucepan. Add water and cold coffee. Cook over high flame until mixture begins to simmer. Reduce heat, add cover, and allow to cook 10 minutes. Serve immediately. Especially good when served with chunks of French bread and herb butter; dessert: fresh strawberries.

Variation: Hearty beef stew: omit zucchini, pepper, eggplant and water chestnuts; add potatoes, carrots, green beans and peas to vegetable/meat mixture in saucepan. Allow to cook for 30 minutes until these vegetables become tender. Reserve tomato. Add to saucepan 15 minutes before serving. Serves 2. To serve 4: Double meat, vegetables, seasoning; use same amount of wine, coffee, gravy, but add ½ cup of water.

Diane M. Grady
Philadelphia, PA

14 Carrot Cold

Preparation time: 45 minutes, plus chilling time

3 tablespoons butter
1½ cups onion, finely
   chopped
1 celery stalk with leaves,
   finely chopped
12 ounces carrots
   (approximately 14 baby
   carrots) cut in ¼-inch
   rounds
2 medium potatoes,
   peeled and diced

1 teaspoon sugar
1 tablespoon chopped
   fresh dill (or 1 teaspoon
   dried)
3 cups chicken broth
1 cup milk
1 cup heavy cream
   Pinch cayenne pepper
   Salt and white pepper
   to taste
   Chopped fresh parsley

Melt butter in 3-quart saucepan. Add onion and celery and saute until onion is translucent. Add carrots, potatoes, sugar, dill and broth. Cook, covered, on low heat 25 minutes. Cool slightly and puree in blender or food processor, one fourth at a time. Cover and chill (or freeze for later use). Just before serving, add milk, cream, cayenne, salt, and pepper. Garnish with parsley. Serves 8. May also be served hot.

Barbara Rondinone
La Crescenta, CA

Gazpacho

Preparation time: 10 minutes, plus chilling time

8 cups tomato juice
6 tablespoons salad oil
4 tablespoons wine vinegar
1 teaspoon salt
1 teaspoon sugar
1 medium cucumber, chopped fine
1 medium to large onion, chopped fine
1 green pepper, chopped fine
2 cloves garlic, minced
2 tablespoons finely chopped parsley
¼ teaspoon pepper
½ teaspoon Worcestershire sauce
1 large tomato, chopped fine
Garnish: croutons, chopped pimiento, diced avocado, onion, green pepper, cucumber

Combine all ingredients in a large bowl. Mix well. Cover and refrigerate overnight before serving. Garnish with croutons and choice of chopped vegetables. Yield: 8-10 cups.

Note: Gazpacho is better if made at least one day in advance and will keep for several days in refrigerator.

Darlene E. Frank
Allen Park, MI

Green Tomato-Aliee

Preparation time: 1½ hours

2 pounds stew beef, with
a small piece of suet
1 tablespoon oil
4–5 green tomatoes, diced
7 ripe tomatoes, diced
1 cup whole kernel corn
1 cup cut green beans
4 medium potatoes,
scrubbed and diced
2 carrots, diced
2 ribs celery with green
tops, cut into small bits
1 very small head
cabbage, cut up

3 medium onions, diced
1 green pepper, cut into
4 pieces
1 small red pepper, cut
into 4 pieces
1 cup ketchup
2 tablespoons sugar
1 bay leaf
1–2 dashes oregano
Salt and pepper to taste
1 cup elbow macaroni

Brown the beef in one tablespoon oil, lower heat, and let
simmer about 20 minutes. In a large pot, heat 2-3 quarts
water and add all the vegetables, ketchup, meat, suet, bay
leaf, oregano, salt and pepper. Cover and simmer until
meat is tender, 40-50 minutes. Add the macaroni and
simmer 10 minutes longer, until macaroni is tender, stirring often to keep it from sticking. Makes 5-6 quarts.

Carol Frakes
Boston, MA

Ham and Lentil Soup

Preparation time: 1½ hours

One ham bone with
ham still on it
2 quarts water
1½ cups lentils, washed
1 bunch scallions,
chopped coarsely
3 carrots, chopped
coarsely (scrub them but
don't scrape them, you
lose valuable nutrients
that way)

3 stalks celery, including
leaves, chopped coarsely
1 tablespoon thyme or
rosemary
Salt and pepper to taste

Simmer ham bone in water for 1 hour. Then add the lentils, chopped vegetables, and seasonings to the stock and simmer gently another 30 minutes. This soup is very versatile. You can include almost any vegetable (squash, beans, mushrooms) or perhaps a can of tomato sauce, as well as leftovers from your refrigerator.

Like many soups, this is even better the next day. It freezes well too.

Christine Valenza
Alameda, CA

Hearty Potato Soup

Preparation time: 1 hour

¼ cup oil	1 teaspoon salt
½ cup chopped onions	⅛ teaspoon dill seeds
2 carrots, diced	Dash cayenne
½ cup chopped celery	½ teaspoon caraway seeds
2 large potatoes, diced	1 cup instant milk powder
2 cups stock	

Heat oil in 2 quart frying pan, dutch oven or crock pot. Saute onions, carrots, celery, and potatoes until onions are transparent. Add stock, salt, and seasonings. Bring to boil, cover and simmer 45 minutes. Dissolve milk powder in 1½ cups soup liquid. Return to pot and simmer 1 minute. Serve hot with beer and crackers. Makes 2 hearty servings.

Linda Ciosek
Hoffman Estates, IL

Mushroom Soup

Preparation time: 45 minutes

3 tablespoons butter	3½ cups chicken broth
½ pound sliced fresh mushrooms	1 egg yolk
	1 cup sour cream
¼ teaspoon caraway seed	1 teaspoon dill
1 tablespoon flour	Salt and pepper

Saute butter, mushrooms, and caraway seeds, sprinkle flour over this and stir well. Add chicken broth and simmer 30 minutes. Beat egg yolk and add it to sour cream and dill. Pour hot broth over sour cream mixture in tureen. Season with salt and pepper. Serves 4.

(49)

Sharon England
St. Clair Shores, MI

New England Clam Chowder

Preparation time: 40 minutes

¼ pound salt pork, diced
1 large finely chopped
  onion
1 cup boiling water
3 medium diced potatoes
1 teaspoon salt

¼ teaspoon pepper
2 cans (8 ounces each)
  minced clams
2 cups milk
1 cup light cream
  Thyme

Fry salt pork in skillet until brown and crisp, remove and drain on paper towels. Saute onion in remaining fat until golden and clear. Add water, potatoes, salt and pepper; cover, simmer until potatoes are tender. Add clams with liquid; heat. Add milk and cream; season to taste. Simmer until ready to serve; do not boil. Serve in bowls topped with salt pork and dash of thyme. Serves 6.

Toby Grossman
Wayne, NJ

Onion Soup Gratinee

Preparation time: 40 minutes

4–5 large onions, minced
3 tablespoons butter
¼ teaspoon fresh ground
  pepper
1 tablespoon flour
3 cans (10½ ounces each)
  condensed beef broth

3 cups water
1 bay leaf
6–8 slices French bread,
  toasted
½ cup grated Swiss cheese

Slice and mince onions. Heat butter in heavy sauce pan over medium heat. Add onions and pepper. Cook, stirring frequently till onions are light brown. Sprinkle onions with flour. Cook 1 minute, stirring constantly. Add beef broth, water and bay leaf. Bring to boil. Simmer 30-40 minutes. Discard bay leaf. Correct seasoning. Turn soup into oven proof soup tureen. Place toast slices on top. Sprinkle with cheese. Place under broiler or in 400° oven until cheese turns golden. Serves 6 to 8 people.

Susan Gail Reinhart
Fullerton, CA

Sheddar Sheese Shoup

Preparation time: 30 minutes

¼ cup butter
¼ cup thinly sliced green onion
3 tablespoons flour
3 cups chicken broth
½ cup each diced celery and carrot

2 cups sharp Cheddar cheese
1 cup milk
¼ cup dry or cream sherry
½–1 cup diced leftover cooked ham or chicken
Pepper to taste

Melt butter in 3-quart pan over medium heat. Add onion and cook 2-3 minutes. Stir in flour; cook 3 minutes. Add broth slowly and cook, stirring, until thickened. Add celery and carrots, cover, cook 15 minutes until vegetables are tender. Stir in cheese and milk and cook until cheese is melted. Blend in sherry and meat; season to taste with pepper. Makes 7 cups. Serve with a dollop of sour cream.

Paul R. Sexton
San Francisco, CA

Vegetable Soup

Preparation time: 2 hours

6 pounds meaty beef shank, salted and peppered

3 tablespoons vegetable oil

1 green pepper, diced

2 stalks celery, thinly sliced

3 medium yellow onions, thinly sliced

3 carrots, thinly sliced

2 large cans (28 ounces each) whole tomatoes (I squish them with a potato masher)

½ cup red wine

1 bay leaf

¼ teaspoon Worcestershire sauce

½ teaspoon Kitchen Bouquet

Salt and pepper to taste

4 ears of corn (slice off kernels)

3 zucchini, thinly sliced

1 pound fresh peas

3 potatoes, diced small

1 pound mushrooms

Any other vegetables you really like (I add broccoli, cauliflower, and green beans in small amounts)

Saute beef in a small amount of oil *slowly* (at about 225° in an electric skillet) until well browned on all sides. Add next 10 ingredients, bring to boil, and simmer, covered, for 45 minutes or until meat is done. Add remaining ingredients. I like soup very thick. If you feel additional liquid is required, add chicken broth to taste. Bring to boil and simmer ½ hour or until vegetables are barely done. Makes 16 or more hearty servings.

Elaine Poffenroth
Edmonds, WA

Wilted Lettuce Soup

Preparation time: 35 minutes

2 slices bacon
6 leaves of leaf lettuce,
    torn in pieces
2 green onions, sliced thin
½ cup whipping cream
¼ cup milk
1 egg, unbeaten

1 tablespoon vinegar
¼ cup boiling water
¼ teaspoon salt
2 pinches of pepper
2–4 small boiled potatoes,
    hot

Fry bacon until crisp. Wash lettuce leaves while bacon is frying. Remove bacon from pan and saute onions in bacon fat until tender. While onions are cooking, combine cream, milk, egg; add vinegar last. When onions are done, add boiling water, salt and pepper to pan and stir. Turn off heat. Add cream mixture and lettuce leaves to pan. Turn heat to very low and stir-cook with a big salad fork until mixture becomes thick and creamy. *Do not boil.* Crumble bacon on top. Serve over boiled white poatoes in soup bowls. Use more vinegar and salt to your preference. An electric fry pan is good to use because it controls the heat better. Recipe serves 2. May be prepared and refrigerated and heated the next day.

Entrées

An entree may be meat and potatoes—or tuna in a hefty baked potato, as in this contest prize winner for main dishes, Hot Baked Po-Tunas. Debra Graveline of Houston, Texas baked this one up. The cooking talents of this busy Kelly temporary employee also won her first prize for a dessert recipe in a local newspaper contest. Other entree selections include delicious curries and stews, all versatile choices for happy dining.

Margaret Kayajanian
Fowler, CA

Armenian Botlijohn (Eggplant)

Preparation time: 1 hour, 45 minutes plus 10 minutes
broiling time

1 large eggplant or two
medium size (enough
to cover bottom and
second top layer of pan)
Margarine or butter
Olive oil or corn oil
2 medium onions,
chopped
1 green pepper, chopped
Parsley, chopped
Garlic salt or powder

Salt
4 garlic cloves, chopped
1 pound ground beef or
lamb
2 cans (8 ounces each)
tomato sauce
Black pepper
Paprika
Oregano
Sweet basil

Cut eggplant in round thick slices and salt each side of
eggplant and soak in water 20 minutes or wash and soak
5 minutes salted on each side with garlic salt or salt.
Meanwhile, heat margarine or butter and oil, and saute
onions, chopped green pepper, chopped parsley, adding
garlic salt, table salt and garlic cloves. In another frying
pan, brown ground meat (just enough to brown) then
add tomato sauce (1 can), black pepper, paprika, sweet
basil, then add the sauted onions, green pepper mixture.
Cook over low heat 45 minutes (covered). In the mean-
time, drain water out of eggplant, sprinkle each side
with black pepper, salt, garlic salt (little) and brush with
margarine or butter (melted) and broil each side of sliced
eggplants until slightly golden (do not overbroil). Place
½ the sliced eggplant in the bottom of a rectangular pan
for one layer, then add the meat sauce, and on top of
meat sauce place remaining sliced eggplant, pour a little
olive oil or corn oil on eggplant (or brush on) then add
the remaining can of tomato sauce, spreading over eggplant to cover. Bake at 350° uncovered ½ hour, then cover
with aluminum foil and bake additional ½ hour. Makes
6 servings.

Irene Spencer
Baltimore, MD

Asparagus and Onion Pie

Preparation time: 1 hour

1½ pounds fresh asparagus	⅛ teaspoon black pepper
3 tablespoons butter	⅔ cup grated Cheddar
2 tablespoons finely chopped onion	cheese
	¾ cup heavy cream
4 large eggs, lightly beaten	1 cup milk
	2 unbaked 8-inch pie shells
1 teaspoon salt	

Cut asparagus into ½-inch pieces. In frying pan melt butter, add onion and saute over low heat until golden. In large bowl combine eggs, salt and pepper, grated cheese, cream, milk, sauted onion and asparagus. Gently mix and pour into pie shells. Bake in 425° oven for 10 minutes; reduce temperature to 325° and bake for 30-40 minutes or until firm in center. Serve immediately. Makes 8 servings.

Trish Cascardi
Cambridge, MA

Beef Carbonade

Preparation time: 2 hours

2 pounds boneless chuck, cut into cubes	1½ tablespoons flour
	1 cup dark beer
Salt, pepper	1 cup beef broth or bouillon
4 tablespoons vegetable oil	
	1 bouquet garni (parsley, thyme, bay leaf, peppercorns)
1 tablespoon butter	
¼ pound bacon	
1¼ cups chopped onions	1 teaspoon red wine vinegar
½ teaspoon minced garlic	

Pat dry meat. Salt and pepper meat. Heat oil and butter in frying pan. Saute meat until browned on all sides. Remove meat to casserole dish. Saute bacon, onion, and garlic in fry pan until tender. Add bacon, onion, and garlic to meat. Sprinkle meat and onion mixture with flour and cook over medium heat for 5 minutes. Add salt and pepper to taste. Add beer and broth or bouillon. Remove from heat and add bouquet garni. Bake at 325° for 1½ hours. Remove fat and reduce sauce until it is thick (5 to 10 minutes). Add red wine vinegar. Serve with rice or noodles. Makes 6-8 servings.

Betty A. Morey
Mobile, AL

Beef Stroganoff

Preparation time: 18 minutes

½ tablespoon flour	1 tablespoon butter
¼ teaspoon salt	1½ tablespoons flour
½ pound beef sirloin, cut in ¼ inch wide strips	½ tablespoon tomato paste
1 tablespoon butter	¾ cup beef stock or canned condensed beef broth
½ cup thinly sliced mushrooms	
¼ cup chopped onion	½ cup dairy sour cream
1 small clove of garlic, minced	1 tablespoon cooking sherry

Combine flour and salt; dredge meat in mixture. Heat skillet, then add butter. When melted, add the sirloin strips and brown quickly, flipping meat to brown on all sides. Add mushroom slices, onion and garlic; cook 3 or 4 minutes or till onion is barely tender. Remove the meat and mushrooms from skillet. Add 1 tablespoon butter to pan drippings; when melted, blend 1½ tablespoons flour. Add tomato paste. Slowly pour in cold meat stock; cook, stirring constantly, until mixture thickens. Return meat and mushrooms to skillet. Stir in sour cream and sherry. Heat briefly. Serve with parsley rice or noodles. Makes 2 servings.

Mary L. Hardesty
Chula Vista, CA

Beef with Raisin Sauce

Preparation time: 1½ hours

1 pound round steak, 2
  inches thick
2 cloves garlic, thinly
  sliced
1 tablespoon vegetable
  oil
½ teaspoon salt
Pinch of marjoram

2 to 3 tablespoons water
1 tablespoon butter
⅓ cup raisins
2 small tomatoes, skinned,
  chopped, and well
  drained
Pickled chilies

Make small, deep incisions in the meat, using a sharp knife; stuff with slices of garlic. Brown meat in oil in heavy skillet. Add salt, marjoram and water. Cover tightly; simmer 1 hour, or until tender. If liquid cooks away, more may be added to prevent scorching. Meanwhile, melt butter in small skillet. Add raisins; saute 10 minutes. Add tomatoes and heat through. Place steak on heated platter. Add raisin sauce to drippings in meat skillet; blend together. Pour over steak; garnish with chilies. Makes 2 servings.

Susan Braly
Portland, OR

Braised Ginger Pork

Preparation time: 30 minutes

1 pound lean 1-inch pork cubes
Flour
1½ tablespoons peanut oil
¼ cup chicken broth
½ cup soy sauce
1 tablespoon sherry
⅛ cup chopped green or yellow onion

½ small clove garlic, crushed
1 teaspoon sugar
2 teaspoons ground ginger
Dash pepper
Hot cooked rice

Dip meat in flour. Heat oil in large fry pan. Add all of meat and brown quickly, remove and set aside. Pour off remaining oil from pan. Combine chicken broth, soy sauce, and sherry. Add onion, garlic, sugar, ginger and pepper. Place in cooking pan along with meat. Simmer, covered for 15 minutes, or until meat is tender. Serve over rice. Serves 2-3.

Ann DeVito
Montreal, Canada

Broiled Shrimp with Garlic Sauce

Preparation time: 30 minutes

1 pound large fresh or frozen shrimp
¼ cup butter
¼ cup oil
1 tablespoon lemon juice
¼ cup chopped shallots

1 tablespoon finely chopped garlic
½ teaspoon salt
Black pepper
¼ cup finely chopped fresh parsley

Shell shrimp and remove vein. Wash and dry with paper towels. Preheat broiler. In shallow baking pan, large enough to hold one layer of shrimp, melt butter over low heat. Do not let it brown. Stir in oil, lemon juice, shallots, garlic, salt and pepper. Add shrimp and turn them in mixture until well-coated. Broil 3 to 4 inches from heat, about 5 minutes, turn and broil 5 minutes longer until slightly browned and tender but firm. Do not overcook. Transfer shrimp to serving platter, pour sauce over and sprinkle with parsley. Serve with steamed rice. Makes 2 servings.

Cathy Payne
Philadelphia, PA

Cathy's Crab Cakes

Preparation time: 1 hour

1 large onion or 2 medium	Salt to taste
½ cup of chopped celery	1 egg
½ cup of chopped green pepper	12 ounces to 1 pound of fresh or frozen crabmeat
2 tablespoons butter	2 tablespoons butter
1 cup of thick white sauce (see recipe below)	Bread crumbs
	Oil for frying

Saute onion, celery and pepper in 2 tablespoons of butter. Add these ingredients to the white sauce. To this add the crabmeat; then beat up 1 egg and add to rest of ingredients. Chill thoroughly in the refrigerator for approximately ½ hour. When thoroughly chilled, shape into crab cakes and roll in bread crumbs. Fry in deep oil over moderate heat until brown. Makes approximately 12 to 15 crab cakes. May be frozen for later use.

Thick White Sauce

3 tablespoons butter
4 tablespoons flour

¼ teaspoon salt
1 cup milk

Melt butter in a saucepan, add flour and cook till smooth; add milk and stir to thick paste.

Eleanor Burger
Annapolis, MD

Cheeseburger Pie

Preparation time: 35 minutes

Cheese Topping:

1 egg
¼ cup milk
½ teaspoon each salt, mustard

½ teaspoon Worcestershire sauce
6 ounces grated cheese

Beat egg, milk and add seasoning. Mix well with cheese.

Filling:

½ to ¾ pound ground beef
¼ cup chopped onions
¼ teaspoon oregano
¼ cup green pepper (chopped)
½ teaspoon salt

½ cup bread crumbs
¼ to ½ cup tomato sauce (according to consistency liked)
1 9-inch pie shell, unbaked

Brown beef in skillet slightly. Skim excess fat. Add all remaining ingredients except pie shell. Mix well and cook just until meat is brown. Place in pie crust. Spread cheese topping over filling. Bake at 425° for 25 minutes, or until cheese topping is bubbling. Can serve with remainder of can of tomato sauce, heated. Makes 3-4 servings.

Mary Eileen Flutka
Rosedale, MD

Cheesy Swiss Steak

Preparation time: 1 hour, 15 minutes

2 pounds round steak,
   about 1 to 1½ inches
   thick
4 tablespoons flour
1 tablespoon salt
⅛ teaspoon pepper
4 tablespoons butter
8 ounces shredded
   mozzarella cheese

2 small onions, sliced
2 carrots, sliced
2 stalks celery, sliced
1 can (8 ounces) tomato
   sauce
1 teaspoon Worcestershire
   sauce
½ bay leaf

Trim fat from beef and cut into serving size portions. Mix flour, salt and pepper and coat beef. Heat butter in skillet and brown meat on both sides. Transfer to 1½-quart buttered casserole as browned. Sprinkle cheese on top of steak. Add vegetables, tomato sauce and seasonings to casserole. Cover and bake in a preheated oven at 350° about 1 hour or until meat and vegetables are tender. Makes 4 to 6 servings.

You may want to serve with mashed potatoes.

Syndy Garza
Carrollton, TX

Chicken Breasts in Wine

Preparation time: 30 minutes

½ stick butter
   Green onion, chopped
4 chicken breasts
   Salt and pepper to taste
½ cup Marsala wine
1 cup heavy cream

2 cans (4 ounces each)
   whole mushrooms or 1
   cup fresh
1 teaspoon paprika
   Sliced ripe olives

In a skillet, heat butter and saute green onion. Add chicken seasoned with salt and pepper, and cook until meat is slightly brown on both sides. Add wine, cream, mushrooms, paprika, and olives. Cook covered until chicken is tender, approximately 20 minutes. Serves 4.

Jacqueline Faye Vincent
Syracuse, NY

Chicken Paris for Two

Preparation time: 1 hour

Two full chicken breasts
    skinned and cleaned
1 teaspoon basil
1 bay leaf
2 teaspoons salt
1 teaspoon black pepper
1 medium head broccoli,
    divided into spears
2 medium onions, sliced
4 tablespoons butter,
    melted
2 fresh tomatoes, skinned
    and quartered
¼ pound Swiss cheese,
    diced
½ pint light cream

Simmer chicken with basil, bay leaf, 1 teaspoon salt and ½ teaspoon pepper for 25 minutes. Remove meat from bones and place in bottom of covered baking dish.

Simultaneously, steam broccoli with sliced onions, 1 teaspoon salt, ½ teaspoon pepper for 10 minutes. Do not overcook broccoli; keep firm.

Remove vegetables from steamer and place on top of chicken, pour melted butter over top. Arrange tomatoes artistically on top and cover with cheese. Pour cream over casserole and bake covered for 25 minutes at 350°.

Serving suggestion: White wine, loaf French bread, tossed salad.

Patricia Futterleib
Bristol, CT

Coffee-pot Chicken

Preparation time: 2-2½ hours

1½ cups diced potatoes
½ cup diced carrots
1 onion (small)
3 tablespoons butter
½ teaspoon soy sauce
½ teaspoon salt
½ teaspoon lemon-flavored pepper
1 roasting chicken (about 2½-3 pounds)

¼ teaspoon chili powder
¼ cup butter
⅓ cup minced onion
1 teaspoon ginger
1 clove garlic, minced
½ cup hot strong coffee
½ cup whipping cream

Saute potatoes, carrots and onion in 3 tablespoons of butter, in 9-inch skillet over medium low heat, stirring frequently, 8 minutes. Add soy sauce, salt and pepper. Rinse chicken, pat dry. Fill cavities with potato mixture, truss chicken. Sprinkle with chili powder. Heat ¼ cup of butter in Dutch oven over medium high heat. Brown chicken well on all sides. Turn breast side up. Sprinkle onion, ginger and garlic around chicken. Pour in coffee, add cream. Heat to boiling. Reduce heat to low, simmer covered, basting occasionally, until tender, 1½ to 2 hours. Remove chicken, cover to keep warm. Increase heat to high. Heat sauce to boiling, stirring constantly, until thickened, 3 to 5 minutes. Strain. Serve sauce with chicken. Serves 2 to 4.

Constance Sanders
Wilton, CT

Connie's Chicken Sauteed

Preparation time: 1 hour

1 pound boneless, skinless chicken breasts (4 half breasts)
¼ pound chilled butter or margarine
Salt, pepper, oregano, chopped parsley
1 cup flavored bread crumbs
½ tablespoon butter or margarine
1 large onion, cut in rings

½ medium green pepper, cut in strips
1 firm tomato, cut in small pieces
1 cup sliced mushrooms (optional)
½ cup ham or cold cuts cut in strips
½ cup sour cream
4 slices Swiss or mozzarella cheese

Place chicken between pieces of waxed paper and pound thin. Do not split flesh. Remove paper. Cut butter into finger-shaped pieces. Place in middle of each breast. Springle with salt, pepper, oregano, chopped parsley. Roll, covering butter completely with flesh. Dredge each piece in bread crumbs. Lightly brown pieces in heated 2 table-spoons butter in skillet. Drain on paper towel. Place in buttered open casserole in 300° oven for 25 minutes (or until done). In same skillet, saute lightly the onion rings, green pepper, tomatoes, mushrooms, ham strips. Stir in ½ cup sour cream. Pour over chicken. Place slices of cheese on each piece and place under a hot broiler just long enough to melt cheese. Serve at once. Makes 4 servings.

Christine Ramsey
Columbus, OH

Corn Pone Pie

Preparation time: 45 minutes

½ pound ground beef
¼ cup chopped onions
¼ cup chopped green
  pepper
¼ cup kidney beans
½ cup canned tomatoes
  (cut up)

1 teaspoon Worcestershire
  sauce
1 teaspoon chili powder
⅔ cup self-rising corn
  meal
⅔ cup milk
1 egg

Brown ground beef, onions and pepper, in a large skillet. Drain off excess grease. Add kidney beans, tomatoes, Worcestershire sauce and chili powder. Heat to boiling, stirring occasionally. Grease a 1½-quart casserole. Pour in ground beef mixture. Combine corn meal, milk and egg. Pour evenly over beef mixture. Bake at 425° for 20 minutes or until corn bread is golden brown. Makes 2 servings.

Barbara Knight
Newark, DE

Crab Pie

Preparation time: 1 hour

3 eggs
1 pound crab meat
1 cup milk
1 cup chopped celery
½ onion, chopped
¼ cup chopped green
  pepper
1 teaspoon dry mustard

1 teaspoon Worcestershire
  sauce
½ teaspoon black pepper
⅛ teaspoon Tabasco
Salt to taste
½ pound saltine crackers,
  crushed
¼ pound butter, melted

Beat eggs well and mix in remaining ingredients, reserving ½ cup cracker crumbs and 2 tablespoons butter for topping. Put mixture into a well greased 1½-quart baking dish. Stir together reserved crumbs and butter and sprinkle over top. Bake at 350° about 45 minutes, until set and brown. Makes 6 servings.

Marolee Ann Collins
San Francisco, CA

Cream and Chicken

Preparation time: 1½ hours

2 large chicken breasts, skinned and boned
Prepared bread stuffing with cracked pecan pieces

¼ cup flour
½ teaspoon salt
¼ teaspoon paprika
Garlic salt
½ cup melted butter

Stuff chicken and close with toothpicks. Roll in flour and seasonings, dip in melted butter. Bake uncovered at 350° for ¾ hour, then lower and bake at 250° for ½ hour (turn once during baking).

Sauce:

½ pound fresh mushrooms (halved)
¼ cup minced onion
2 tablespoons flour
½ cup heavy cream

½ cup sour cream
½ teaspoon salt
¼ teaspoon pepper
Pecan pieces

Cook mushrooms and onion in the remainder of the ½ cup butter till tender. Remove mushrooms. Stir flour into butter, add cream, sour cream, salt and pepper, and heat slowly to boiling point. Add mushrooms, stir. Pour over chicken. Sprinkle with pecans.

Bettie Wilke
Canton, OH

Deviled Hamburgers

Preparation time: 20 minutes

½ pound hamburger
⅙ cup chili sauce
¾ teaspoon mustard
¾ teaspoon horseradish
½ teaspoon minced onion

¾ teaspoon Worcestershire
 sauce
½ teaspoon salt
2 or 3 hamburger buns
 Bit of melted butter

Combine all ingredients except buns and butter. Cut buns in half and spread with meat mixture. Brush with melted butter and place in broiler for about 10 minutes, 5 to 7 inches from heat, until cooked through. This is incredibly simple and totally different from the usual hamburger. One pound will easily make 6 sandwiches for a get-together and that's really as inexpensive a recipe as you'll ever find! Recipe is rather bland without horseradish; however, so try to have that on hand.

Yolanda Weeks
Addison, IL

Duckling a l'Orange

Preparation time: 2½ hours

1 duckling, 3-4 pounds
1 teaspoon salt
¼ teaspoon black pepper
2 tablespoons orange juice
¾ cup brown sugar,
 packed

4 teaspoons orange peel
½ teaspoon dry mustard
¼ teaspoon allspice
⅛ teaspoon ginger
2 tablespoons flour
2 cups orange juice

Clean duckling. Rub inside cavity and outside of duckling with mixture of salt and pepper. Remove wing tips to first joint. Fasten neck skin and wings to back of duckling with skewers. Close the cavity opening with skewers and tie legs together. Place on rack in roasting pan, breast side down. Roast in 450° oven for 30 minutes. Reduce temperature to 350° and turn duckling so breast side is up. Continue roasting, allowing 30 minutes per pound. The last 30 minutes of cooking time begin basting with mixture of the 2 tablespoons orange juice, brown sugar, 3 teaspoons of the orange peel, dry mustard, allspice and ginger. (For less crisp skin, start basting last 15 minutes.) Continue basting with drippings from pan until the duckling is tender and skin is crisp and brown. Remove to platter and keep hot. Pour off grease, leaving only brown drippings. Stir flour and the remaining 1 teaspoon orange peel into pan drippings. Add the 2 cups orange juice and cook over low heat until thickened, stirring constantly. Strain into sauce dish and serve with hot duckling. Serves 2-3.

Jenny Materyn
Canton, MI

Easy Pirogi

Preparation time: 45 minutes

6 lasagne noodles	½ cup shredded Cheddar
1 pound cottage cheese	(or American) cheese
1 egg yolk	2 tablespoons butter or
Onion salt to taste	margarine, softened
1½ cups mashed potatoes	Salt and pepper to taste

Cook noodles as directed on package. Drain and allow to sit in cool water to keep from sticking. In buttered 9x5x3 inch loaf pan, lay down 2 noodles lengthwise. Combine cottage cheese, egg yolk and onion salt. Pour in over noodles for first layer. Set in 2 more noodles. Combine mashed potatoes, Cheddar cheese and 1 tablespoon butter. Layer over noodles. Pat gently in place. Top with last 2 noodles, dab with butter. Cover and place in 375° oven for ½ hour. Uncover, turn off oven, and let sit for 5 minutes to steam dry slightly. To serve, cut in squares and enjoy with cold sour cream. Serves 4 for lunch or 2 for supper.

Joan Serino
Rome, NY

Empanadas

Preparation time: 1 hour

For filling:

1 tablespoon diced onion	½ cup cooked peas or other vegetable
2 tablespoons butter	
½ cup diced tomato	1 hard boiled egg, chopped
½ cup water	
Salt and pepper to taste	2 tablespoons raisins
1 cup cooked chicken or or other cooked meat	1 or 2 tablespoons of bread crumbs (optional)

For pastry:

2 cups of flour	½ teaspoon salt
2 teaspoons baking powder	1 cup heavy cream
	Oil for frying

Preparation for filling: Lightly fry the onion in butter and add the tomato; then add the water, seasonings and meat; cook for a short time until warm; then add remaining ingredients and remove from heat.

Preparation for pastry: Mix dry ingredients and add cream slowly a little at a time; form into a soft dough that can be kneaded by hand. Divide into 16 parts and roll into ¼ inch thickness; handle gently. Add filling and fold over, sealing edges well. Heat oil in bottom of frying pan and cook until browned lightly on both sides. Place on paper towels to absorb excess oil. Makes 16.

Note: A pastry mix may be used to quicken preparation. Almost any cooked meat and vegetable combination may be substituted.

Sherry Gebis
Chicago, IL

Fettucine

Preparation time: 15 minutes

10-ounce package of
   medium-size noodles
3 ounces butter
½ pint sour cream
½ pint heavy (whipping)
   cream

4 ounces grated Parmesan
   cheese
2 tablespoons finely
   chopped chives
Sprinkling of nutmeg
Salt and pepper to taste

Cook and drain noodles well. Melt butter and add noodles. Blend in sour cream. Stir a minute or two over low flame. Add heavy cream. Cook slowly for 5 minutes. Add cheese, nutmeg and chives. Stir until cheese melts. Serves 4.

Diane F. Burke
Tallahassee, FL

Fish Gumbo

Preparation time: 1 hour

- 1 medium onion, chopped
- 1 medium green pepper, chopped
- 1 tablespoon margarine
- 2 cans (16 ounces each) tomatoes
- 1 bay leaf
- 1 teaspoon celery salt
- ½ teaspoon leaf thyme, crumbled
- 1 dried red pepper, crushed
- 1 can (16 ounces) cut okra
- 1 pound bass or other fish fillets, cubed

Saute onion and green pepper in the margarine in a sauce pan for 5 minutes. Add tomatoes, salt, celery salt, bay leaf, thyme, and red pepper. Bring to boil and simmer uncovered about 30 minutes. Add okra and fish. Simmer about 30 minutes or until fish is cooked. Remove bay leaf. Serve on cooked rice. Makes 4 servings.

Lorraine Janssen
Holland, MI

Fish in Champagne

Preparation time: 60 minutes

- 4 fish fillets
  Fresh ground pepper
- 1 small white onion, sliced thin
- 2 bay leaves
- 1 split of champagne (or 1 cup white wine)
- 1 tablespoon butter or margarine
- 1 tablespoon flour
- 2 teaspoons dill
- 1 lime, sliced

Place fish fillets in shallow baking dish. Sprinkle with pepper. Add onions, bay leaves, and champagne. Cover with foil and refrigerate several hours or overnight. To cook, place covered baking dish in preheated 325° oven, for 15 to 35 minutes, depending on thickness of fillets. While fish is poaching, melt butter over low heat in a small saucepan. Add flour and dill and stir into a paste. Remove fish from oven and slowly pour half the champagne drippings over the paste and stir over low heat until it thickens, about 2 to 3 minutes. Gently lift fish onto platter and spoon sauce over it. Garnish with lime slices. Serves 2-4.

Gary E. Kidd
Bloomfield Hills, MI

Gary's Blue Cheese Chicken

Preparation time: 1 hour

2 whole chicken breasts, halved and boned
Salt
Flour
1 egg, beaten
Bread crumbs
2 tablespoons butter
2 tablespoons oil
1 pint sour cream
½ pound blue cheese, crumbled
4 cloves garlic, pressed

Salt chicken, then dip in flour. Next dip chicken in beaten egg, then in bread crumbs. Brown slightly on both sides in the butter and oil.

Arrange in a shallow baking dish. Mix together in a medium size bowl the sour cream, blue cheese and garlic. Pour this mixture over the chicken. Bake, covered, at 350° for 45 minutes. Serves 4.

Note: This recipe is quite rich, which is due to the sour cream and the blue cheese. Use your discretion when pouring cheese mixture over chicken.

Karen Feinberg
Cincinnati, OH

Gourmet Chicken Livers

Preparation time: 20-25 minutes

1 cup cooked rice, white
  or brown
8 ounces chicken livers
½ cup flour
½ teaspoon salt
¼ teaspoon pepper
¼ teaspoon garlic powder

3–4 tablespoons margarine
1 garlic clove or shallot
½ cup white wine
  Pinch of basil
1–2 tablespoons tomato
  paste

Keep rice warm while doing the following: Cut livers into bite-size pieces. Mix flour, salt, pepper, and garlic powder and spread mixture on plate. Coat pieces of liver in mixture. Melt margarine in skillet. While margarine is melting, mince the garlic or shallot. Lightly brown liver and garlic or shallot in margarine. Add wine, basil, and tomato paste and stir gently to mix. Cover skillet and simmer 5-10 minutes. Serve on rice. Serves 2.

Alaka Karandikar
Alameda, CA

Ground Beef Curry

Preparation time: 40 minutes

1 pound ground beef
1 medium size onion,
  finely chopped
4 tablespoons oil
¼ teaspoon turmeric
¼ teaspoon ground
  cinnamon
¼ teaspoon ground cloves
¼ teaspoon black pepper

¼ teaspoon ginger
1 teaspoon curry powder
2 cloves garlic, crushed
½ teaspoon salt
1 can (8 ounces) tomato
  sauce
16 ounces water
½ cup frozen green peas

Brown beef and drain off fat. In large skillet on medium heat saute onion in oil until brown. Combine turmeric, cinnamon, cloves, black pepper, ginger, curry powder, crushed garlic, salt, and add to skillet. Add ground beef, tomato sauce, water, frozen green peas. Stir, cover and simmer for 20 minutes. Stir occasionally. Makes 2 servings. Serve with rice or bread.

Joanne Stone
Brentwood, MO

Guacamole Tacos

Preparation time: 20 minutes

1 medium onion, chopped
2 tablespoons vegetable oil
1 can (1 pound) tomatoes
1 tin (4 ounces) roasted, chopped green chilies
¼ teaspoon ground cumin
½ teaspoon salt
⅛ teaspoon oregano

2 avocados, mashed
⅓ cup chopped scallion
2 tablespoons lemon juice
2 teaspoons ground cumin
1 clove of garlic, minced
½ teaspoon salt
8 taco shells
1½ cups shredded lettuce
¾ cup shredded cheese

Saute onion in oil until softened. Add next 5 ingredients and simmer 10 minutes. Combine avocado, scallion, lemon juice, 2 teaspoons cumin, garlic, and ⅛ teaspoon salt. Fill taco shells with avocado mixture, spoon tomato mixture over, and sprinkle with lettuce and cheese. Makes 8 servings.

Dorothy Marie Loving
Richmond, VA

Ham Souffle in Green Pepper Cup

Preparation time: 25 minutes

2 large green peppers
2½ ounces ham, diced
6 tablespoons skimmed milk
½ tablespoon butter or margarine

1½ tablespoons all purpose flour
½ teaspoon prepared mustard
2 slightly beaten egg yolks
2 egg whites

Place peppers on side, remove slice from the side. Scoop out seeds and pulp. (Save slices for other recipes.) Cook peppers in boiling salted water for about 5 minutes. Drain and set aside. Meanwhile in blender combine ham, milk. Cover and blend until ham is slightly chopped. In a small saucepan melt butter or margarine, stir in flour and mustard, add ham-milk mixture and cook until thickened. Remove from heat and gradually beat mixture into egg yolk. Beat egg whites until stiff, fold into yolk mixture. Spoon into peppers, place in baking dish and bake for about 25 minutes at 375° until set. Serves 2.

Debra Graveline
Houston, TX

Hot Baked Po-Tunas
(Tuna-Stuffed Baked Potatoes)

Preparation time: 45 minutes

4 hot baked potatoes

Filling:

- 1 cup mayonnaise (not salad dressing)
- ½ cup grated Cheddar cheese
- ¼ cup chopped green peppers
- ¼ cup chopped pimientos
- ¼ cup chopped green onions
- 2 cans (7 ounces each) solid pack white tuna, drained

Topping:

- ¼ cup mayonnaise
- 2 tablespoons grated Cheddar cheese
- 1 egg white, stiffly beaten

Scoop baked potato from shells. Lightly toss scooped out potato with filling ingredients. Spoon back into shells. Heat 10 minutes at 400°. For topping fold ¼ cup mayonnaise, 2 tablespoons grated Cheddar cheese into 1 egg white, stiffly beaten. Spoon over hot stuffed potatoes. Heat an additional 10 minutes until lightly brown. Makes 4 servings.

Margaret L. Laughton
Ormond Beach, FL

Hot Chicken Salad

Preparation time: 30 minutes

1 cup cooked chicken chunks
1 cup seasoned poultry stuffing
2 tablespoons mayonnaise
1 can (4 ounces) mushrooms, drained
1 rib celery, diced
1 small carrot, diced
1 tablespoon green pepper, chopped

1 small pimiento, cut in small strips
¼ teaspoon salt
¼ teaspoon pepper
¼ teaspoon garlic powder
1 tablespoon lemon juice
2 tablespoons sharp cheese, grated
1 tablespoon wheat germ

Preheat oven to 375°. Mix all ingredients except wheat germ. Place in small casserole, 1-quart size or less. Lightly grease casserole if necessary. Do not cover. Sprinkle with wheat germ. Bake until bubbly, about 15 minutes. Serves 2.

Theo Ann Wille
St. Charles, MO

Irish Stew with Dumplings

Preparation time: 5 hours in crock pot

- ¾ pound beef (stew meat, if small beef portion is unavailable)
- ¾ cup flour, about
- Salt
- 2 tablespoons fat (shortening)
- ⅛ cup diced carrot (1 small size)
- ⅛ cup diced turnip (1 small size)
- ⅛ cup diced onion (1 small size)
- ¾ cup diced potato (1 medium)
- Few grains pepper
- 2½ cups boiling water

Cut beef in cubes; dredge with flour and ¼ teaspoon salt. Brown meat in fat. Add carrot, turnip, onion, potato, water, ¼ teaspoon salt and pepper into crock pot. Add browned beef. Do not stir. Cover, simmer. Cooking time can depend on if your area has high to low extremes of humidity. (For example, St. Louis vs. Phoenix.) When meat is tender, remove meat and vegetables from crock pot. Mix 3 tablespoons flour to 3 tablespoons water (plus dashes of salt and pepper) in a cup until the mixture resembles paste. Stir into liquid in crock pot. You may add 1 teaspoon instant coffee at this point—no taste—but it makes the gravy brown. When liquid is heated, return meat and vegetables to crock pot, stirring occasionally.

*Dumplings:

- ½ cup flour
- ¼ teaspoon salt
- ¾ teaspoon baking powder
- ¾ tablespoon shortening
- ¼ cup milk

Sift dry ingredients together. Cut in shortening. Gradually add milk; mix until smooth. Drop by tablespoons on hot stew. Cover. Cook last hour.

* Dumplings for two is enclosed as Master Mix recipe.

(79)

Deborah Butkovich
Hillsboro, OR

Italian Pot Roast

Preparation time: 2½ hours

4 pounds pot roast	2 onions, chopped
½ teaspoon salt	1 large carrot, sliced
½ teaspoon pepper	1 cup tomato juice
2 cloves garlic, cut into slivers	½ teaspoon basil
	2 teaspoons oregano
½ cup flour	1 cup tomato puree
¼ cup olive oil	

Rub meat with salt and pepper. Make tiny, deep incisions on all sides of the meat with the point of a knife and push a sliver of garlic into each cut. Roll meat in flour. Heat olive oil in deep, heavy pot and, over high heat, brown meat on all sides. While meat is browning, peel and chop onion, scrape and slice carrot, and measure out other ingredients. When meat is brown, lower heat and add tomato juice, carrot, onion, basil, and oregano. Cover and simmer gently for 1¼ hours.

After 1¼ hours, add tomato puree and stir through. Simmer for 35 minutes longer. Remove from heat and serve. Cooking time 2 hours. Serves 6. This dish may be served with mashed potatoes. When preparing and mashing the potatoes, add sour cream for an added taste. Also as a vegetable: fresh string beans boiled until almost done—remove from heat and drain. Add olive oil and fresh clove of garlic, chopped. Continue cooking until done.

Lianne Moccia
Chapel Hill, NC

Linguine al Cavolfiore

Preparation time: 30 minutes

- 2 tablespoons olive oil
- 1½ cups cauliflower, broken into 1-inch flowerets
- 2 medium cloves garlic, crushed
- 1 bay leaf
- 1 teaspoon basil
- 1 cup tomato puree or 1 cup tomato sauce
- ½ teaspoon salt or more to taste
- ¼ teaspoon black pepper
- ½ pound linguine, uncooked
- 1 tablespoon butter
- 1 cup of mixed grated Parmesan (or Romano) and Cheddar cheese

Heat 1 teaspoon olive oil in a frying pan. Add garlic, bay leaf and basil. Saute for 2 minutes, then add cauliflower and sprinkle it with salt and pepper. Saute for several minutes more, add tomato puree or sauce, lower heat and simmer 20 minutes. Cook the linguine according to the directions on the package. Drain, toss with remaining olive oil (1 tablespoon), butter and half the cheese. Spread onto a large platter, pour sauce on top, and spread with remaining cheese. Serve at once. Makes 4 servings.

Doug Weiskopf
Portland, OR

Luau Ribs

Preparation time: Approximately 2 hours

2 *pounds meaty spareribs*

Sauce:

1 *jar strained baby food peaches*
¼ *cup catsup*
¼ *cup vinegar*
1 *tablespoon soy sauce*

¼ *cup brown sugar*
1 *clove garlic, minced*
½ *teaspoon ginger*
½ *teaspoon salt*
Dash pepper

Sprinkle both sides of meat with salt and pepper. Place ribs, meat side up in foil-lined shallow pan. Bake in very hot oven, 450°, 15 minutes. Remove excess fat. Mix all ingredients for sauce together. Pour sauce over ribs. Continue baking in moderate oven 350°, 1½ hours, or until done, basting with sauce several times. Cover it through entire roasting time. Makes 2 servings.

Sally Lorenz
South Daytona, FL

Manicotti

Preparation time: 35 minutes

Shells

4 eggs
Salt to taste
1 cup water

1 cup sifted flour
1 tablespoon oil

Filling

½ pound browned ground
beef (optional)
2 cups ricotta cheese
¼ cup mozzarella cheese,
diced
2 teaspoons grated
Parmesan cheese

2 eggs, well beaten
1 teaspoon salt
Dash of pepper
1 quart jar of tomato
sauce

To make shells, beat together eggs, salt, water and sifted flour, until real smooth. Then in hot oil make up about 12 pancakes.

Mix together the beef (if used), all the cheeses, eggs and salt and pepper, until smooth. Fill each pancake with cheese mix and roll. Prepare 3 1-quart baking dishes by putting some tomato sauce in to cover the bottom. Place 4 rolled pancakes in each pan. Cover with the remaining sauce and sprinkle with grated Parmesan. Bake at 350° for about 45 to 60 minutes. Each pan serves 2. The other 2 pans should be covered and frozen. When you are ready to use frozen manicotti, just take a pan from freezer and put in refrigerator in the morning before work and when you get home, all you have to do is reheat, and they're better than the fresh ones!

Londa Minarich
St. Charles, MO

Meat Sauce and Noodle Casserole

Preparation time: Approximately 1 hour

2 ounces medium noodles,
cooked and drained
½ pound ground beef
1½ teaspoons butter or
margarine
2 tablespoons minced
onion
¼ to ½ teaspoon garlic salt
½ teaspoon salt
Dash of pepper

1 can (6 ounces) tomato
paste
Water
¼ cup dairy sour cream
¼ cup cream style cottage
cheese
¼ cup shredded Cheddar
cheese

Cook noodles according to package directions. Meanwhile, brown beef in butter. After meat begins to brown, add onions and garlic salt. Saute until meat is well browned, stirring occasionally. Add salt and pepper and mix thoroughly. Drain excess fat from meat. Stir in tomato paste and enough water to make a sauce of medium consistency. Let simmer until noodles are ready. Combine sour cream and cottage cheese. Combine cooked and drained noodles with sour cream and cottage cheese. Mix well. In greased 1-quart casserole bowl, layer meat mix and noodle mix alternately starting with the meat mix and ending with the noodle mix. Top with shredded cheese. Place in 350° oven for about 20-30 minutes, until casserole is hot and the shredded cheese melts. Makes 2 servings.

Helpful hints: Make 2 meals at one time! Double all ingredients and divide equally into two 1 quart bowls. Place one in the freezer for a later date and heat one now for immediate use. (Frozen one is *not* heated in the oven prior to freezing and will require 50-60 minutes heating time at 400°.)

Company coming in the middle of the week? The weekend prior to their arrival, prepare recipe doubled or trebled according to the number of guests. Freeze until needed. Be sure to allow enough time for casserole to become thoroughly heated (400° for 60 minutes or more, according to amount made). Serve with a large salad, preferably made the night before, and you have a complete meal with little or no kitchen clean up before your guests arrive.

Becky Eastwood
Vancouver, WA

Mexican Chicken Tortillas

Preparation time: 45 minutes

- 6 corn tortillas
- ¼ cup oil
- 2 cooked chicken breasts, diced (cook by stewing for ½ hour in 2 cups water and 1½ teaspoons salt)
- 1 cup sour cream
- 1 tablespoon garlic salt
- 1½ teaspoons chili powder
- 1 teaspoon each salt and ground pepper
- 1½ teaspoons cumin
- ½ can (4.2 ounces) chopped ripe olives
- 1 small can (4 ounces) diced green chilies, drained
- 1½ cups shredded Monterey Jack cheese
- ¼ cup sliced green onion
- 1 cup shredded Cheddar cheese

Optional:

- ¾ cup shredded lettuce
- ½ cup chopped tomato
- ½ cup guacamole

Fry tortillas in hot oil for 6 to 10 seconds on each side. Set aside. Stir together chicken, sour cream, garlic salt, chili powder, salt, pepper, cumin, olives, chilies, Jack cheese, and green onions. Spoon about ½ cup of the chicken mixture down the center of each tortilla. Roll up to enclose. Place tortillas seam side down in a single layer in a shallow 8x8x2-inch baking pan. Cover and chill, if made a day ahead. Bake, covered, in a 375° oven until hot, about 20 minutes if at room temperature, about 30 minutes if chilled. Remove cover and sprinkle evenly with the Cheddar cheese; return to oven and bake, uncovered, until cheese melts, about 3 to 5 minutes. Makes 2 servings. You can serve with shredded lettuce, chopped tomato, and/or guacamole. Sprinkle over each serving.

Mrs. Helen M. Haaland
Woodbury, CT

Misty Isles Eggplant

Preparation time: 30-40 minutes

1 clove garlic
¼ teaspoon salt
1 tablespoon shortening
½ pound chopped beef or lamb
1 small onion, chopped
1 small eggplant, washed, dried and diced

1 teaspoon lemon juice
1 teaspoon salt
½ cup tomato juice
4 tablespoons raisins
¼ cup sour cream
Minced parsley or chives

Rub bottom of heavy skillet with cut cloves of garlic and salt. Add shortening and heat. Add meat and onion and fry gently, stirring to fry evenly. Add eggplant. Sprinkle with lemon juice. Add salt and tomato juice and blend well. Add raisins and cover pan. Simmer for fifteen minutes. Add sour cream and heat through. Sprinkle with greens before serving. Great over toasted bread or mashed potatoes! Makes 2-3 servings.

Janette B. Dalton
Buffalo, NY

Monterey Chili Con Carne

Preparation time: 50 minutes

½ pound ground beef
½ cup chopped onion
1 clove garlic, minced
1 can (8 ounces) tomatoes, cut up
1 can (8 ounces) kidney beans

1 teaspoon chili powder
½ teaspoon ground cumin
⅛ teaspoon salt
¼ cup water
¼ cup cubed Monterey Jack cheese (¼ inch cubes)

Brown ground beef with onion and garlic in Dutch oven, about 5 minutes. Drain off fat. Add tomatoes, kidney beans, chili powder, cumin, salt and water. Simmer, covered 35-40 minutes. Serve sprinkled with cheese. Makes 2 servings.

Joan P. Strickland
Powell, TN

Mushroom-Cheese Quiche

Preparation time: 1 hour

1 9-inch pie shell
2 tablespoons oil
½ onion, chopped
½ cup chopped mushrooms (canned may be subsituted for fresh)
1 cup shredded cheese

4 ounces cream cheese
4 eggs, beaten
1 cup milk
1 teaspoon basil
½ teaspoon marjoram
⅛ teaspoon salt
1 green pepper, sliced (optional)

Bake pie crust at 450° for 5 minutes. Place oil in a skillet on medium heat and add mushrooms and onions. Saute about 4 minutes. Sprinkle onion, mushrooms and cheese on the bottom of the pie shell. Soften cream cheese by putting it in a bowl set in hot water. Combine softened cream cheese and the rest of the ingredients (except green pepper). Beat until smooth. Pour into shell. Gently place pepper slices on top of custard. Place pie in a preheated 450° oven and reduce heat to 375°. Bake until an inserted knife comes out clean, about 35 minutes. Serves 4.

Rose Ledwidge
Troy, MI

Mushroom Pie

Preparation time: 1 hour

1 cup chopped onion
3 tablespoons margarine
1½ pounds sliced fresh mushrooms
1½ teaspoons Worcestershire sauce
1 teaspoon salt
½ pound shredded Swiss cheese
1 9-inch unbaked pie shell

Saute onion in margarine for about 2-3 minutes. Add mushrooms, Worcestershire and salt. Cook 5 minutes. Drain well. Add cheese and stir. Bake in pie shell at 375° for 35-40 minutes.

Kathleen A. Rader
Austin, TX

Natural Sweet and Sour Chicken

Preparation time: 40 minutes

Batter:

⅓ cup whole wheat pastry
flour
⅓ cup oat or rice flour
¾ cup water
⅓ cup hulled sesame seeds

1–2 tablespoons soy sauce
(to taste)
1 teaspoon Italian
seasoning
½ teaspoon cinnamon

Sweet and Sour Sauce:

2 tablespoons frozen
orange juice concentrate
2 tablespoons cider
vinegar
2 tablespoons orange
blossom honey
1 teaspoon stone ground
mustard

2 tablespoons soy sauce
1 teaspoon natural
turmeric
½ teaspoon powdered
ginger

Chicken and Vegetables:

2 chicken breasts
8 fresh mushrooms
¼ green pepper
½ onion

½ small carrot
10–15 snow peas
½ cup sesame seed oil

Combine batter ingredients in order, stirring until batter
is of a pourable consistency. Combine sauce ingredients
in order in a small saucepan, stir well, and place over
low heat and let simmer 5 minutes. Simmer chicken in
water until cooked. Drain, skin, bone, and cut into small
pieces. Cut mushrooms, pepper, onion, and carrot into
thin slices. Cut tops off snow peas. Heat oil in skillet

or wok. Dip chicken pieces in batter and quickly stir-fry. As chicken is browned, drain on paper towels and place in a serving bowl. Place all of vegetables in pan and quickly stir-fry. Pour vegetables into bowl with chicken. Pour sauce over mixture. May be served with rice. Makes 2 servings.

Jack A. Duncan
Gardendale, TX

Oyster-Shrimp Jambalaya

Preparation time: 1 hour

2 tablespoons olive oil
4 green onions, chopped
2 large onions, chopped
½ pound smoked sausage, cubed
½ pound pickled meat, cubed
1 pound can whole tomatoes, chopped
½ cup chopped celery
1 bay leaf
3 pounds peeled and washed shrimp
1 pint oysters
4 cloves garlic
1 tablespoon parsley, chopped
2 cups raw rice
2–3 cups water
2 chicken bouillon cubes
Salt, pepper to taste
Hot pepper sauce to taste

Heat olive oil and saute the onions until brown with pickled meat and sausage. Add tomatoes and cook to brown. Add celery, bay leaf and fry this down about 10 minutes. Add shrimp, oysters, garlic, parsley and rice and cook a few minutes, stirring often to fry rice a little. Now add 1 cup of water, chicken bouillon cubes and cover the pot. Cook until the rice is done, adding a little water at a time as needed. Add salt and pepper to taste. Remove bay leaf before serving. Serve hot if possible, but this is good warmed over the next day. Makes 8-10 servings.

Esther Blum
Baltimore, MD

The Pasha's Curried Chicken with Peanut Sauce

Preparation time: 45 minutes

¼ cup peanut oil
3 pounds chicken breasts, skinned and boned, cut into bite-sized pieces
1 medium onion, minced
1 clove garlic, pressed
1 cinnamon stick, broken
1 tablespoon good curry powder
¾ teaspoon ground ginger
2 large tomatoes, skinned and chopped or 1 can (16 ounces) tomatoes, cut up

¾ cup plain yogurt
1 tablespoon chopped fresh parsley
½ teaspoon sugar
½ teaspoon salt
6 tablespoons peanut butter

Heat oil in large heavy skillet. Brown chicken pieces slightly and remove from pan. Add onion and garlic and saute until tender. Reduce heat and add spices and cook until flavors develop. Stir in remaining ingredients except the peanut butter and blend well. Return the chicken to the skillet and turn pieces to coat evenly. Cover and simmer 30 minutes or until chicken is tender. Remove the chicken and boil down the sauce until thick. Stir in peanut butter. This dish can be prepared a day in advance and reheated at 350° for 30 minutes. Serve 4-6. Excellent with saffron rice.

Rocio de la Cantera
Tallahassee, FL

Picadillo

Preparation time: 20 minutes

A

1 onion, chopped
½ green pepper, chopped
2 garlic cloves

1 tomato, chopped
3 Spanish olives

B

½ teaspoon of oregano
¼ teaspoon capers
2 teaspoons olive oil

2 ounces tomato sauce
1 teaspoon garlic salt
Salt and pepper

C

1 pound ground beef

D

1 tablespoon red wine
2 ounces dried raisins

Saute ingredients in A, medium high temperature, and
then add group B. Add the meat (C) and brown. Then
add group D. Cover with lid and let cook at medium
heat. Serve over white rice or on a bun. Makes 4 servings.

Wanda Roy
Fort Myers, FL

Pizza Dinner Loaf

Preparation time: 45 minutes

½ pound ground beef
(lean)
½ cup tomato paste
½ cup stewed tomatoes
(optional)
¼ cup sliced canned
mushrooms
¼ cup ripe black olives
¼ cup grated Parmesan
cheese

2 tablespoons chopped
onions
¼ teaspoon oregano
1 very small clove of
garlic, chopped fine
½ loaf long Italian bread,
sliced in half,
lengthwise
9 slices mozzarella cheese

Combine first 9 ingredients. Slightly scoop out center of bread. Spread beef mixture evenly onto each half. Bake in a 425°-450° oven, on the top rack, for 15 minutes. Remove and top with mozzarella cheese. (Cut cheese into 4 triangles.) Return to oven until cheese melts. Makes 2 servings.

Sheila Harrison
Troy, MI

Pork a la Harrison

Preparation time: 1 hour

2 loin pork chops
1½ ounces butter
½ pound mushrooms,
chopped
1 tablespoon lemon juice
¾ ounces flour
Salt, pepper

1 teaspoon dried thyme
2 tablespoons cooking oil
4 tablespoons heavy
cream, lightly whipped
1 tablespoon chopped
parsley

Fry pork chops in butter until golden on both sides; remove, keep hot. Pour off all fat except 2 tablespoons. Add mushrooms. Cook slowly until tender. Add lemon juice and flour. Cook until fairly dry. Add salt, pepper and thyme. Set chops on squares of silver foil; brush with oil. Spoon some mushroom mixture and one tablespoon of cream onto each chop. Sprinkle with parsley, wrap and place in oven at 350° for 35 minutes. Serve with jacket potatoes and green tossed salad. Makes 2 servings.

Roberta Foley
N. Chelmsford, MA

Pork Chops Pierre

Preparation time: 1½ hours

1 small onion	1 tablespoon brown sugar
2 stalks celery	½ teaspoon salt
1 tablespoon butter	⅛ teaspoon pepper
¼ cup water	8 loin pork chops, ½ inch
½ cup ketchup	thick
2 tablespoons vinegar	1 large green pepper,
1 tablespoon lemon juice	seeded, cut into rings
1 tablespoon	1 large onion, sliced into
Worcestershire sauce	rings

Peel and finely chop small onion, celery. Combine butter, onion, celery in a 2-quart saucepan, saute until tender. Add water, ketchup, vinegar, lemon juice, Worcestershire sauce, sugar, salt, pepper. Cover and simmer for 20 minutes. Brown chops on both sides in preheated 10-inch fry pan. Place chops in 9x13 inch bake pan, pour sauce over chops, top with pepper rings and onion slices. Cover with aluminum foil and put into a 400° oven for 45-50 minutes. Makes 8 servings.

Maria Radeka
Spartanburg, SC

Potato Supreme

Preparation time: 45 minutes to 1 hour

2 large baking potatoes
½ cup cooked leftover chicken, ham or pork roast (chopped)
½ cup grated Cheddar cheese

1 small onion—chopped
½ green bell pepper—chopped
¼ cup mushrooms—sliced
4 tablespoons sour cream

Boil or bake potatoes till done; place potatoes on aluminum large enough to wrap potatoes. Slice potato in half lengthwise almost through and open. Place half of the chopped meat on each potato, then the grated cheese; next the chopped onion and bell pepper. Then pat 2 tablespoons sour cream on each potato, and top with the sliced mushrooms. Bring the foil up over the potato, and fold to close. Return to 350° oven for about 15 to 20 minutes. Can be used as a main dish with a salad—or if small potatoes are used, can be used as a vegetable.

Beth Schulman
—Howard Beach, NY

Rolled Cheddar Chicken

Preparation time: 1 hour

2 pounds boneless, skinless chicken breasts
12 ounces sharp Cheddar cheese, grated
1 egg
¼ cup water
Paprika, salt, pepper

1½ cups seasoned bread crumbs
4 tablespoons butter, melted
Oregano, garlic powder, onion powder

Cut whole chicken breasts into halves. Pound chicken breasts with spoon to flatten. Place grated cheese in center of chicken breasts. Roll closed and seal with toothpick. Coating: Mix egg with ¼ cup water, few dashes of paprika, salt and pepper. Spread bread crumbs in flat dish and add ¼ teaspoon each of oregano, paprika, garlic powder, salt, pepper, onion powder. Dip rolled chicken breast in egg solution. Then roll in bread crumbs. Grease 11-inch baking pan. Lay chicken in pan and pour melted butter over chicken. Also add any leftover breadcrumbs and cheese on top of chicken. Bake at 350° for 50-60 minutes (until brown). Serves 4-6.

Helen Robiolio
Union City, NJ

Rolled Veal Cutlets

Preparation time: Approximately 1 hour

4 *veal cutlets*
4 *or 5 sprigs of fresh*
  parsley
1 *clove garlic*
  Salt and pepper to taste
3 *tablespoons butter,*
  about
  Dash of dried rosemary ⎫ *increase quality*
  Dash of dried sage ⎬ *if fresh herbs*
  Dash of dried basil ⎭ *are used*
½ *cup white wine*
  Water, as needed

Flatten veal cutlets. Combine parsley and garlic with salt and pepper; mince well. Spread mixture onto cutlets, roll the meat and seal with a toothpick. Saute cutlets in butter and herbs until brown, adding small quantities of water as needed to prevent meat from sticking to skillet. When cutlets have been browned, turn flame up high and add the wine (with water, if needed). After a few seconds, reduce the flame, cover and let simmer for about 45 minutes, or until tender. Check occasionally to be sure liquid is not drying out, in which case water should be added. Makes two servings. Delicious served with rice, zucchini and a salad of your choice.

Note: Whenever adding liquid, be sure it is poured onto the skillet—never onto the meat itself.

Laurie Ware
Atlantic Beach, FL

Roquefort Pasta Piquante

Preparation time: 10 minutes

- ½ *pound crumbled Roquefort or blue cheese*
- ¼ *cup milk*
- 1½ *tablespoons butter*
- ¼ *cup whipping cream*
- ½ *pound spinach pasta or fettucine, cooked al dente*
- ½ *jar marinated artichoke hearts (optional), sliced lengthwise*
- ¼ *cup freshly grated Parmesan cheese*

Combine Roquefort or blue cheese, milk and butter in large saucepan; place over low heat and stir until smooth. Add cream and stir until sauce is well blended. Add pasta (which is still hot), artichoke slices and Parmesan cheese and toss until noodles are well coated. Serve immediately with additional Parmesan if desired. Serves 2-4.

Patricia Mahnich
Boise, ID

Savory Chicken and Potato Stew

Preparation time: 1 hour, 15 minutes

1 small onion (chopped)	1 can chicken broth
¼ cup celery (chopped)	⅓ cup white cooking wine
¼ cup butter or margarine	(omit if desired)
4 pieces of chicken (parts	½ cup water
to your liking, see note)	2–3 medium potatoes,
1 tablespoon garlic salt	diced
Pinch of rosemary	2 tablespoons shortening
leaves (more can be	
added to taste)	

Brown onion and celery in butter. Add chicken pieces, garlic salt and rosemary leaves. Brown chicken till gravy is brown and chicken begins sticking. Add ½ can chicken broth, wine and ½ cup water. Simmer till chicken is very tender (about 45 minutes). Save remaining chicken broth. (An electric fry pan works very well for this.) Brown diced potatoes in shortening, using a frying pan with a lid, until tender and brown. About 10 minutes before serving, add potatoes to above chicken. Add remainder of chicken broth and ½ cup water. Bring to boil, then turn down to simmer for about 10 minutes. Skim off excess fat. Serves 2.

Note: 1 pound of beef stew can be substituted for chicken —cook same way. To increase for larger crowd just add more chicken (or beef) and potatoes.

Anne Howard
Burlington, MA

Seafood Special

Preparation time: 20 minutes

1 package (8 ounces)
frozen langostinos,
thawed

1 can (4½ ounces) shrimp,
drained

½ stick (¼ cup) butter

1 pint fresh mushrooms,
sliced or 1 can (4
ounces) sliced
mushrooms, drained

4 tablespoons flour

1 bottle (8 ounces) clam
juice

½ cup evaporated milk

2 tablespoons pimiento,
chopped

1 tablespoon chives,
chopped
Salt and pepper, to taste

1 tablespoon sherry
(optional)

4 patty shells, cooked
according to package
directions

Drain langostinos and shrimp on paper towel. Saute
them in butter for 5 minutes. Add mushrooms and saute
5 minutes longer. Sprinkle with flour and stir constantly
over low heat until well blended and smooth. Slowly
add clam juice and milk, stirring constantly, until mixture becomes thick and smooth. Add pimiento, chives,
salt, pepper, sherry and blend well. Serve on patty shells.
Makes 2 servings.

Roseann Kalich
Salinas, CA

Skirt Steak Supreme

Preparation time: 30 minutes

2 tablespoons onion, finely chopped
½ teaspoon oil
1 teaspoon milk
½ teaspoon red wine
¼ teaspoon Worcestershire sauce
⅛ teaspoon garlic powder
⅓ teaspoon parsley flakes
⅓ cup seasoned croutons
Water as necessary
1 skirt steak, skinned and cut lengthwise
Salt and pepper as desired

Saute chopped onion in frying pan with oil until brown. Add milk, wine, Worcestershire sauce, garlic powder, parsley flakes, and heat for a few minutes. Then add croutons and enough water to make pasty. Take a skirt steak and cut lengthwise in half. (Each steak will serve two people.) Spread the above onion mixture on the steak, and then roll the steak and fasten with toothpicks. Salt and pepper to taste. Broil steak for 5 minutes and then turn over and broil another 5 minutes or until done. (Use regular size broiling pan.)

Serve this steak with French onion soup, green salad, baked potatoes, and string beans. Serves two people.

Lynn F. Martini
Kenner, LA

Slow-Cooking Spaghetti Sauce

Preparation time: 30 minutes plus cooking time

1 tablespoon margarine	12 ounces water
1½ pounds ground beef, lean	1 can (8 ounces) of mushrooms, drained
1 large bell pepper, finely chopped	2 tablespoons parsley flakes
½ large onion, finely chopped	1 heaping tablespoon brown sugar
3 stalks celery, finely chopped	1 teaspoon ground oregano
2 cans (16 ounces each) whole tomatoes, cut up	1 teaspoon basil leaves
1 can (15 ounces) tomato sauce	1 teaspoon salt
1 can (12 ounces) tomato paste	½ teaspoon garlic powder
	¼ teaspoon black pepper
	2 whole bay leaves

In a large skillet, melt margarine. Brown ground beef, separating pieces of meat with fork, over medium heat. Drain off excess fat. In a slow-cooking pot, combine browned meat along with the rest of the ingredients. Stir and mix well. Cover and cook on high for 8 to 10 hours. Serve over hot spaghetti. Top with grated Parmesan cheese. Serve with hot, crusty bread and a crisp, green salad for a delicious meal. This recipe makes 8 to 10 servings, but you can use whatever amount you need and freeze the rest of the sauce in a tightly covered container for use on another day. Just reheat and serve over hot spaghetti. This sauce fits well into a working schedule as it can be prepared before work in the morning, allowed to cook all day, and served for dinner that night. Or the onion, bell pepper, and celery can be cut up and the meat can be browned and refrigerated overnight so that all ingredients will be ready to put together in the slow cooker in the morning, thus saving even more preparation time.

Jill A. Kamholz
Melbourne Beach, FL

Snapper Rolls Elegant

Preparation time: 36 minutes

3½ tablespoons butter or margarine
¼ cup chopped onion
1½ ounces canned chopped mushrooms
4 ounces crabmeat (drained if canned)
¼ cup coarsely crushed saltines
1 tablespoon parsley, snipped

Salt and pepper to taste
1 pound red snapper fillets (4 fillets)
1½ tablespoon flour
Milk
¼ cup dry white wine
2 ounces shredded Swiss cheese (about ½ cup)
¼ teaspoon paprika

In a skillet melt 2 tablespoons butter and cook onion until tender. Drain mushrooms, reserving liquid, and stir into onion with crab, crushed saltines, parsley, salt and pepper. Remove skillet from heat and mix well. Lay out fillets and spread crab mixture over them. Roll up fillets and place seam side down in a small casserole. In a saucepan, melt 1½ tablespoons butter and add flour. Add enough milk to mushroom liquid to make ¾ cup. Add this to flour mixture with wine. Stir to blend over low heat. Cook until thickened, stirring occasionally. Pour over fillets. Cook covered for 20 minutes in 350° oven. Sprinkle with cheese, recover, and put in oven for 5 more minutes. Garnish with paprika. Makes 4 servings.

Kay Wietkowski
Houston, TX

Sole Gratin with Mushrooms

Preparation time: 1 hour

1½ pounds sole fillets
⅓ cup dry white wine
2 tablespoons lemon juice
Salt
4 tablespoons butter
½ pound sliced
mushrooms (save 4 or 5
for garnish)

3 tablespoons flour
½ cup half-and-half or
milk
⅛ teaspoon nutmeg
¾ cup shredded Swiss
or gruyere cheese

Arrange sole fillets side by side in shallow casserole no less than ⅓ inch nor more than 1 inch thick. Pour in wine and 1 tablespoon lemon juice; salt fillets. Cover and bake 400° for 8-10 minutes until fish flakes with a fork. Measure juices; if less than 1 cup, add water; if more than 1 cup, boil down. Cover and chill fish; reserve liquid. Melt 2 tablespoons butter in skillet. Add mushrooms and 1 tablespoon lemon juice. Cook on high until mushrooms are limp and juice evaporated. Set aside. Melt remaining 2 tablespoons butter. Stir in 3 tablespoons flour. Remove from heat and gradually stir in reserved 1 cup fish broth, half and half and nutmeg. Return to heat and cook until thickened. Add mushrooms to sauce. Pour sauce over fish fillets, sprinkle with grated cheese and bake in 400° oven for 10 minutes or until bubbly and cheese is browned. Sprinkle with ground nutmeg and serve.

Note: This dish may be prepared ahead of time, refrigerated, and cooked the next day. Makes 4 servings.

Ladson, SC
Connie Laubenthal

"Something Different" Meat Loaf

Preparations time: 70 minutes

½ pound ground beef
⅓ cup milk
⅓ cup graham cracker crumbs
⅛ cup catsup

⅛ cup onion, chopped
½ teaspoon salt
Dash pepper
1 egg

Mix together all ingredients in a large bowl. Shape into a loaf or pack into a baking dish. Top with additional catsup and slices of onion for a special touch. For a juicier meat loaf add more milk or catsup to taste. Bake in a 350° oven for 1 hour. Serves 2 people.

Janet B. Carlson
Clarkston, GA

Southern Corn Bread and Beef Casserole

Preparation time: 30 minutes

¾ pound ground beef (lean)
¼ cup chopped onion
1 can (8 ounces) tomato sauce (you may wish to reserve ⅛ cup for topping)
2 or 3 fresh sliced mushrooms or very small can mushrooms (optional)

½ teaspoon salt
⅛ teaspoon pepper
¾ cup corn bread mix (either from box or package)
½ teaspoon caraway seed (optional)
1 egg, beaten
¼ cup milk

Heat oven to 425°. Cook beef and onion in a small skillet until lightly browned. Stir in tomato sauce, mushrooms, salt and pepper; heat until mixture bubbles. Pour into a 1-quart greased baking dish. Combine corn bread mix, caraway seed, egg and milk. Drop batter onto hot beef mixture by tablespoons. Spread evenly over beef. Bake for 15 to 20 minutes. Cut into squares and serve topped with reserved tomato sauce. Garnish with green pepper rings, if available, or parsley. Makes 2 generous servings.

Carol Evans
Los Angeles, CA

Spaghetti Pie

Preparation time: 50 minutes

6 ounces spaghetti (3 cups cooked)
2 tablespoons butter
⅓ cup Parmesan cheese
2 well-beaten eggs
1 pound ground beef
½ cup chopped onions
¼ cup green pepper
1 can (6 ounces) tomato paste

1 can (16 ounces) tomatoes
½ teaspoon sugar
½ teaspoon crushed oregano
½ teaspoon garlic salt
Parmesan cheese

Cook spaghetti according to package directions. Drain water and stir in butter, cheese and eggs. Form mixture into a 10-inch buttered pie plate. In skillet cook meat, onions, green pepper until meat browns. Drain off fat. Add paste, tomatoes (chopped), sugar, oregano, and garlic salt. Heat thoroughly; mixture should thicken. Fill pie plate with this and bake uncovered at 350° for 20 minutes. Sprinkle with Parmesan. Serves 2 to 6.

Scott Buchanan
San Jose, CA

Squid: Poor Man's Abalone

Preparation time: 25 minutes

1 pound whole squid	1 teaspoon paprika
1 cup bread crumbs	Cooking oil
½ teaspoon garlic salt	

Clean squid using this method: Separate body and head/legs in sink. Rinse away internal organs. Be sure you have removed feather-shaped bone. Cut off the legs below the eye and save with the cleaned bodies. Slit the bodies up one side. Hammer the bodies (laid flat) with an abalone hammer if you have one. Cut bodies into ½-inch wide strips. Mix bread crumbs with garlic salt (easy on this) and paprika. Roll squid strips and legs in crumbs. Put ½ inch of oil in pan bottom and heat until just smoking. Fry squid in hot oil for about 30 seconds. For the body strips this is when the meat turns white. For legs, this is when they have finished curling. For fancy occasions the legs may be eliminated or saved. Serves 2. Round out the meal with rice, fresh green salad and burgundy.

Norene Wessel
Clarksville, IN

Steak a la Norene

Preparation time: 15 minutes

2 cube steak, ½ inch thick	1½ tablespoons lemon juice
½ teaspoon dry mustard, salt and fresh ground pepper to taste	1 teaspoon snipped chives
	½ teaspoon Worcestershire sauce
2 tablespoons butter or margarine	6–8 fresh mushrooms, sliced

Sprinkle one side of each steak with ¼ of the mustard and some salt and pepper. Pound with mallet. Repeat on other side with balance of mustard, salt and pepper. Melt butter in heavy skillet, add steaks, cook two minutes on each side at very high heat. Place on platter and keep warm. Add lemon juice, chives and Worchestershire sauce and bring to boil. Reduce heat and add mushrooms till heated through. Spoon sauce over steaks and serve. This is a fast and simple to prepare dish with a touch of elegance. It is meant to be served and eaten immediately. It does not keep, and still maintain its fine flavor and texture.

Pamela E. Sayre
Tacoma, WA

Stir Fry

Preparation time: 40 minutes

¾ pound top round or sirloin steak
⅛ cup vegetable oil
1 small onion, sliced
¾ cup diagonally sliced celery
½ cup thinly sliced carrots
1½ teaspoons cornstarch
⅓ cup soy sauce

1 can (4 ounces) tomato sauce
½ teaspoon sugar
⅛ teaspoon ground ginger
1 small green pepper, cut in thin strips
2 ounces fresh mushrooms, sliced
1½ cups hot cooked rice

Trim steak and cut into thin strips 2 inches long. Sear in oil in skillet or wok over high heat. Separate onion slices into rings and add to skillet with sliced celery and carrots. Stir and fry just until crisp and tender. Blend cornstarch with soy sauce in small bowl and stir in tomato sauce and seasoning. Add all at once to skillet with green pepper strips and mushrooms. Stir and fry 3-4 minutes longer until sauce thickens slightly and becomes shiny. Serve on hot cooked rice. Make 2 servings.

Martha S. Rau
Louisville, KY

Stuffed Cabbage Casserole

Preparation time: About an hour

- 1 medium-sized head of white cabbage
- 1 pound ground chuck
- ½ cup uncooked quick oats
- 1 egg
- 1 medium-size onion, cubed
- ¼ cup catsup
- 1 teaspoon oregano
- ½ teaspoon salt
- ¼ teaspoon pepper
- 4 strips of bacon
- 1 tablespoon bread crumbs

Slice cabbage in half and parboil in salted water. Remove from water, let drain and set aside to cool. Meanwhile, combine ground chuck with next 7 ingredients and mix very well. Form into round patty. Any quart size baking dish with cover will serve well. Lay two strips of bacon across bottom of baking dish. Cover with cabbage leaves so that part of the leaves reach up the side of the dish and partially over the dish. Line the entire dish in that manner. Lay your meat patty into the lined dish and use the leftover leaves to cover the meal well. Fold the hanging over leaves on top of the covered meat and pat down. Criss cross with the two leftover bacon strips and sprinkle with bread crumbs. Cover. Bake at 350° about 45 minutes, or until top is brown and meat is cooked through. Makes four servings. Serve with potatoes and applesauce.

David A. Striker
St. Louis, MO

Stuffed Italian Zucchini

Preparation time: 40 minutes

1½ tablespoons olive oil
½ pound ground beef
½ cup minced onion
1 garlic clove (minced)
2 eggs, beaten
¼ cup chopped parsley
½ cup Romano or
   Parmesan cheese, grated
1 teaspoon salt
½ teaspoon garlic salt

2 dashes pepper
½ tablespoon Italian
   seasoning
½ teaspoon oregano
1 teaspoon sweet basil
½ tablespoon spaghetti
   sauce seasoning
2 medium zucchini
¼ pound mozzarella
   cheese

To prepare filling, in 10-inch skillet over medium heat, in 1½ tablespoons of olive oil, cook ground beef, minced onion, and garlic clove until meat is browned. Remove from heat and place in medium-sized bowl. Stir in two eggs, ¼ cup minced parsley, and ½ cup Romano cheese. Then season with remaining spices, stirring thoroughly to distribute spices throughout the mixture.

To prepare zucchini, cut each zucchini in half and scrape seeds out, using a spoon. Take filling and place into zucchini shells. Place stuffed zucchini on a cookie sheet, and place in oven, preheated to 350°, for 5 minutes. Then remove from oven and place slices of mozzarella cheese over each zucchini piece. Put back into oven for 5 more minutes or until cheese is melted. Zucchini is then ready to be served. May be served plain or with spaghetti sauce ladled over it. Makes 2 servings.

Polly Ann Petruska
Union Lake, MI

Summertime Zucchini Lasagna

Preparation time: 1½ hours

½ pound mushrooms

1 pound mozzarella cheese, fresh, grated medium

1 small container small curd cottage cheese

3 eggs, beaten

2 teaspoons parsley flakes

½ cup dry bread crumbs

½ cup grated Parmesan or Romano cheese
Dash of onion salt

6 cups zucchini, sliced (with skin)
Note: If squash is large, remove the seed section, which will cause bitterness

2 small garlic cloves
Margarine

1½ pounds ground beef (preferably lean)

1 can (16 ounces) herb-seasoned tomato sauce

1 can (10½ ounces) condensed tomato soup, undiluted

2 teaspoons salt

½ teaspoon oregano

½ teaspoon basil

Preheat oven to 350°. Wash and slice mushrooms, set aside. Grate mozzarella cheese, return to refrigerator. Blend together cottage cheese, eggs and parsley flakes. Return bowl to refrigerator. Mix together bread crumbs and dry Parmesan cheese. Add dash of onion salt. Set aside. Steam zucchini over boiling water about 5 minutes. Drain immediately; cool. Slice garlic cloves very thin and brown in large skillet in small amount of margarine. Make sure to coat the entire surface of skillet with this mixture. Remove garlic; discard. Add ground beef and brown well. Skim off any excess grease. Remove from heat. Add tomato sauce, soup, salt, oregano and basil to meat mixture.

Assembly: Set out all six mixtures and two 8-inch square baking dishes on working counter. Layer the mixtures as follows: First, make one layer of zucchini slices, slightly overlapped. Then sprinkle about ¼ of bread crumb mixture lightly over zucchini. (Use ¼ in the second dish also.) Spoon in a layer of cottage cheese/egg mixture (about ½ inch thick). Use about ½ of mixture in each dish. Lay in fresh mushrooms to cover third layer. Do not overlap. Spoon in ¼ of beef and sauce mixture in each dish, completely covering mushrooms. Lay in a second layer of zucchini, overlapping slightly. Sprinkle with another one fourth of bread crumb mix. Repeat a layer of beef and sauce mix (use half of remaining mix in each dish). Liberally coat top of each baking dish with grated mozzarella. Set baking dishes in oven on foil sheet to catch possible boil-over. Bake 25-35 minutes at 350°. Serve immediately with salad, red wine, and dinner rolls. Makes 8-12 servings.

Alice E. Groh
Mansfield, OH

Swedish Meat Balls

Preparation time: 1½ hours

1 quart beef broth
¼ cup flour
¾ cup cold water
1 pound ground chuck
½ cup chopped celery
1 cup chopped onion
½ cup chopped raw potato
1 teaspoon fresh or dried parsley
½ cup shredded carrots
1 whole egg
1 teaspoon garlic powder

1 teaspoon sherry cooking wine
1 teaspoon salt (or to taste)
½ teaspoon pepper (or to taste)
Dried bread crumbs, if desired
1 tablespoon bacon fat or lard
1 tablespoon flour

In a saucepan, bring to boil the beef broth, and thicken to make a thick, rich gravy by stirring in the flour mixed with the water. Turn fire to low. In a mixing bowl mix the ground chuck, celery, ½ cup onion, potato, parsley, carrots, egg, garlic powder, cooking sherry wine, salt, and pepper together. (For a better flavor let stand one hour.) Form into balls the size of walnuts (or use a meat baller). If they will not hold shape of ball add dried bread crumbs. In a large skillet, add a tablespoon bacon fat or lard. (I use the bacon fat—it gives a better flavor.) Fry the meat balls, turning them gently on all sides until brown. When almost brown, add remaining sherry wine if desired. Remove balls and fry the drippings and onion just a little bit longer. Add a tablespoon of flour, and brown with this mixture; add enough cold water to form a thick gravy. Add the meat balls, and pour over the meat balls the thickened beef broth from before. Season with salt and pepper. Cook slowly for one hour, or bake in the oven between 300° to 350°, covered. (I put the meat balls in a greased glass baking dish and bake them in the oven.) Makes 4 servings. (What's nice about this dish, you can make it the day ahead of time.)

Janet Sinyard
Birmingham, AL

Sweet and Sour Pork

Preparation time: 40 minutes

1 pound boned pork loin cut in squares
3 teaspoons soy sauce
3 tablespoons flour
1 tablespoon cornstarch
1 tablespoon soy sauce
¾ cup chicken broth
1 tablespoon butter
½ cup diced green peppers
3 slices diced canned pineapple, diced
½ teaspoon ginger
¼ cup vinegar
2 tablespoons brown sugar
½ cup pineapple juice
¼ teaspoon salt

To prepare pork for sauce: In a cast iron frying pan, brown the pork loin cut in squares. Dip in soy sauce and then in flour; deep fry until it comes to the surface and floats. For sauce: Combine the cornstarch, soy sauce and chicken broth. Melt the butter and add cornstarch mixture along with green peppers, pineapple, ginger, vinegar, sugar, pineapple juice and salt. Simmer until thickened. Add the browned pork. Serve with rice. Makes 2 servings.

Donna Ingle
Independence, OR

Tangy Tasty Pot Roast

Preparation time: 2 hours

1 small pot roast (2–3 pounds)
2 tablespoons oil or shortening
Garlic salt and pepper
1 small onion, sliced
2 cups water
2 medium red potatoes, whole, unpeeled

2 apples, peeled and quartered
4 whole cloves
2 cups sauerkraut, drained
¼ teaspoon thyme

In electric skillet, brown pot roast on both sides in oil or shortening. Add garlic salt, pepper and onion. Add 2 cups water. Simmer, covered, 1 hour, adding water as needed. Add potatoes, apples, cloves. Spread sauerkraut over all and sprinkle with thyme. Continue cooking until tender, adding water if needed. Serve with green beans and French bread. Serves 2.

Shirley Anne Barrett
Jacksonville, FL

Top Notch Tuna Pie

Preparation time: 30 minutes

1½ cups raw long-grain rice	¾ cup milk
4 eggs, beaten	¼ teaspoon salt
1 can (7 ounces) tuna	¼ teaspoon pepper
1 can (16 ounces) corn	½ teaspoon dried parsley
6 ounces of Swiss cheese, shredded	

Cook rice according to package directions and add two eggs. Put rice into buttered 10-inch pie plate to form a crust. Next layer is can of tuna drained. Next layer is Swiss cheese to cover all of tuna. Next is layer of corn, drained. Take ¾ cup of milk, 2 eggs, salt, pepper, and parsley and beat with a fork. Pour over the pie and bake at 325° for 45 minutes. This recipe fits perfectly into a 10-inch pie plate. If you only have 8-inch pie plates you can make two pies by dividing everything in half except the tuna. You will need to use two cans of tuna, one for each pie. Cook both pies and save one for a later date. Makes 8 servings.

Shelley Vincent
Decatur, GA

Tuna Swirls

Preparation time: 40 minutes

1 cup sifted flour	1 teaspoon sugar
¼ teaspoon salt	¼ cup shortening
2 teaspoons baking powder	1 unbeaten egg
	Evaporated milk

Sift flour, salt, baking powder, and sugar in mixing bowl. Cut in shortening until particles are fine. Combine egg with evaporated milk to measure one half cup. Add egg and milk to dry ingredients all at once. Stir until mixture clings together. Knead on floured surface for 10 strokes. Roll to a 6-inch rectangle.

Filling:

1 can (6½–7 ounces) tuna fish	½ cun shredded cheese
1 small onion, finely chopped	1 well-beaten egg

Mix all thoroughly. Spread evenly on dough. Roll up and cut into slices. Put on ungreased baking sheet 1 inch apart. Bake at 425° for 15-20 minutes. Make white sauce and add cheese. Pour over each. Serves 2-4.

White Sauce (if desired):

3 tablespoons margarine	1½ cups milk ...
3 tablespoons flour	¼ cup grated cheese

Melt margarine. Stir until smooth, adding flour a little at a time. Slowly add milk and stir until boiling. Take off burner and add cheese.

Recipe is excellent for serving a larger group. To serve 8-10, use 2 cups flour, ½ teaspoon salt, 3½ teaspoons baking powder, 2 teaspoons sugar, ½ cup shortening, and combine one egg and milk to measure ¾ cup. Add to dry ingredients. Roll to a 12-inch rectangle. For filling, use 2 cans tuna fish, 1 medium onion finely chopped, the same amount cheese (½ cup), and just one egg.

Nancy Ofiara
Melbourne, FL

Turkish Pilaff

Preparation time: 40 minutes

2½ cups water
2 tablespoons instant beef bouillon
4 teaspoons cinnamon
½ cup pitted prunes, chopped
¼ cup white raisins
¾ cup natural long grain converted rice
1 tablespoon butter
¾ pound ground lamb*
1 large onion, sliced
1 teaspoon freshly ground black pepper
¼ teaspoon curry powder
3 tablespoons fresh lemon juice
3 tablespoons fresh minced parsley
½ cup slivered almonds, lightly browned in 4 tablespoons butter
Salt and pepper

In a heavy saucepan, boil water. Add 1 tablespoon bouillon, 1 teaspoon cinnamon, prunes, raisins, and rice. Cover and cook over low heat until liquid is absorbed (about 20 minutes). While rice is cooking, heat butter, saute lamb, onion, pepper, curry powder, remaining bouillon and cinnamon until mixture is cooked (do not brown). Add rice mixture to meat. Stir in lemon juice, 2 tablespoons parsley (reserve 1 tablespoon), and ¼ cup almonds with butter (reserve ¼ cup almonds). Cover and simmer 5 minutes. Add salt and pepper to taste. Garnish with remaining parsley and almonds. Makes 2 servings.

* Ground beef may be substituted for lamb.

Note: Recipe may be easily doubled.

Stephanie Quinten
Franklin Brunet
Ottawa, Canada

Veal Casserole

Preparation time: 50 minutes

1½ tablespoons cooking oil
1½ tablespoons butter
2 pounds veal steak, cut
  in thin strips
3 tablespoons flour
  Salt to taste
¼ teaspoon pepper
1½ cups water

1 chicken bouillon cube
6 small onions, cut into
  small pieces
½ cup white wine
2 bay leaves or 1 teaspoon
  bay powder
2 tablespoons parsley

In a large pan, heat oil and butter together. Add veal and brown on both sides. Remove veal to a plate. Then blend flour, salt and pepper with the juices left in the pan. Continue stirring, add water and bouillon cube. Lower the heat and add onions, wine, bay leaves and parsley. Put the veal back into the pan and continue to cook over a low heat for about ½ hour or until tender.

Serve with hot rice and corn with cherry tomatoes. Will serve 4 people generously.

Mildred Marks
Brooklyn, NY

Veg-All Tuna Patties

Preparation time: 45 minutes

1 can (7 ounces) tuna fish
1 small onion
1 small zucchini
1 small carrot
1 egg

1 tablespoon milk
½ cup bread crumbs
4 tablespoons oil
2 tablespoons butter

Empty complete contents of can of tuna fish into bowl. Grate in the onion, peeled zucchini, cleaned carrot. Beat egg with the milk, add to the contents of the bowl. With hand chopper, chop until the ingredients are mixed together. Add the bread crumbs. Mix with fork until everything is blended together. Make the patties; if it seems too loose, add more bread crumbs until the patties are solid enough so that they don't fall apart.

Put oil and butter into pan. Heat until just sizzling; add patties and cover. Cook 7 minutes on each side, leaving uncovered the last 2 minutes. The patties should be browned on both side. (You can also use any leftover cooked vegetables for this recipe.) Makes 2 servings.

Patty Cockrell
Seattle, WA

Vegetarian Fried Rice

Preparation time: 20 minutes

1 tablespoon oil
(vegetable or peanut)
⅓ green pepper, diced
3 tablespoons diced onion
⅓ cup grated carrots
3 stalks of Bok-Choy
(Chinese lettuce),
shredded
½ cup tofu (optional)

1 egg (scrambled)
1 teaspoon slivered ginger
(fresh)
1 cup cold cooked rice
(white or brown)
2 tablespoons soy sauce
(add more to taste)
1½ tablespoons sesame or
sunflower seeds

Heat oil in heavy frying pan or wok to 325°-350°. Cut vegetables and tofu into small pieces. Fry egg (scramble). Stir fry vegetables, tofu, ginger, rice, and egg, add soy sauce and seeds. Lower heat and cover, stirring occasionally (about 4 minutes). Serve immediately. Makes 1-2 servings.

Vivian Mortensen
North Vancouver, Canada

Viv's Special

Preparation time: 25 minutes

½ cup diced ham or diced
bacon

1 can (8 ounces), diced
mushrooms, drained, or
1 cup of freshly diced
mushrooms

1 large onion

4 medium-sized eggs

¼ teaspoon pepper

½ cup diced Cheddar
cheese, preferably mild
marble Cheddar cheese

1 medium-sized tomato,
sliced

Use a 9- or 10-inch French Teflon pan, or any other pan
that does not cause food to stick to pan. First fry up diced
bacon or ham, then add mushrooms and onions until mixture is a crisp golden brown. When these ingredients are
almost done, take the 4 eggs along with ¼ teaspoon of
pepper and whip them up in a bowl by hand until foamy.
Remove the cooked ingredients from the pan and set
aside for garnish. Then pour the eggs onto a hot pan and
sprinkle the diced Cheddar cheese over the eggs. When
eggs have turned a golden brown on side facing down
on pan, carefully take a spatula and flip the eggs like a
pancake onto the other side for browning. When the egg
pancake is thoroughly cooked, if desired, you can sprinkle
a bit of Cheddar cheese on top of the egg pancake for
extra cheese flavor. Garnish with diced ham or bacon and
the onions and mushroom mixture and add sliced tomato.
It will look very much like a pizza. Makes 2 servings.

Muriel Wellinghoff
Dellwood, MO

Wellinghoffer's Koenigsberger Klops
(mit noodles)

Preparation time: 45 minutes

(German-Americans' answer to Russian-Americans' stroganoff and Italian-Americans' spaghetti and meatballs.)

3 cups boiling water
2 tablespoons lemon juice
2 bay leaves
3 or 4 cloves
1 tablespoon capers
1 pound ground beef
½ pound ground pork (I use pork sausage)
¾ cup chopped onions
2 eggs

1½ teaspoons salt and pepper (to taste)
2 tablespoons anchovy paste (or 2-ounce can of flat anchovies, chopped fine)
2 tablespoons flour blended with 3 tablespoons cold water
6 ounces egg noddles

Combine first 5 ingredients in a saucepan and bring to a boil. Simmer while making meatballs. Combine beef, pork, onions, eggs, salt and pepper, and anchovies and form into small balls. Add flour to the simmering broth, and then drop meatballs in boiling broth and simmer approximately 10 minutes, rolling them over once or twice to cook through. While these are cooking, boil 6 ounces of egg noodles (medium width) for 15 minutes in 2½ quarts salted water. Drain in strainer or colander and make nests on serving plates, and place 3 or 4 of the meatballs in the nest and spoon some of the hot gravy-type broth over them. Then garnish with 3 or 4 capers.

Note: This recipe makes about 30 meatballs. but extras can be frozen and used in fresh broth any day coming up, and preparation time will be cut in half. Hearty eaters find 5 meatballs is the right serving.

Dolores Damschroder
Oregon, OH

Whole Wheat-Wheat Germ Pancakes

Preparation time: 20 minutes

¾ cup whole wheat flour
¾ cup wheat germ
1 teaspoon salt
2 teaspoons baking
  powder
1 egg, beaten
3 tablespoons melted
  butter

1¼ cups milk
1 tablespoon honey
  Vegetable oil
  Topping: cream of
  coconut, fresh
  strawberries

Mix dry ingredients together, set aside. In small bowl, beat egg and gradually add melted butter, milk, and honey. Stir liquid mixture into flour mixture. Allow to stand 5 minutes. Heat vegetable oil in griddle. Cook about 2-3 minutes, turn only once, and cook other side until done. Top with cream of coconut and fresh strawberries. You may use any topping of your choice. Makes about 14 4-inch pancakes. Batter not used can be kept in refrigerator or you may make all pancakes and re-warm by placing pancakes in tin foil and put in preheated 300° oven for 20 minutes.

You can toss up marvelous salads and dressings from the collection in this chapter, but the winner still comes out Italian Supper Salad. You can *arrange* this supper companion solo-style, as a picture-pretty cold meal. This is the design of Ruth Buechley, of Jacksonville, Arkansas, who joined Kelly Services not long ago, after being away from the work force for 22 years. She loves cooking, was a member of the Officers' Wives Club, and took second prize in the Uncle Ben's Cooking Contest for her rice tabouli salad.

Carolyn Bernfeld
New Rochelle, NY

Anchovy Salad Dressing

Preparation time: 5 minutes

4 anchovies
½ cup olive oil
3 tablespoons wine-
   vinegar
Pepper to taste

Mash anchovies to a paste. Add remaining ingredients.
Mix and serve over green salad. Makes about ¾ cup.

Susan Newton
Austin, TX

Apple Snow Salad

Preparation time: 30 minutes plus time to freeze

1 can (8¾ ounces) crushed
   pineapple, undrained
2 beaten eggs
½ cup sugar
¼ cup water
3 tablespoons lemon juice

Dash salt
2 cups diced, unpeeled
   apple
½ cup chopped walnuts
1 cup whipping cream

In saucepan, combine first 6 ingredients. Cook over low
heat, stirring constantly, till thickened. Chill thoroughly.
Stir in apple and nuts. Whip cream till soft peaks form;
fold into apple mixture. Pour into 8x8x2-inch pan. Freeze
till firm. Let stand at room temperature 10 to 15 minutes
before serving. Cut into squares. Serves 9. This is delicious
as a salad which can be substituted as dessert, but it's
light. You'll want it with lunch, too.

Helen Friend
North Miami Beach, FL

Caponata Salad

Preparation time: 15 minutes plus ½ hour to chill

1 hard-boiled egg
1 can (4¾ ounces)
eggplant appetizer
(caponata)
1 can (6½ ounces) tuna
¼ teaspoon salt
¼ teaspoon pepper

½ medium onion, sliced
thin
4 lettuce leaves, washed
and drained
Red wine vinegar and
.oil dressing

Boil egg night before and put in refrigerator with eggplant appetizer and tuna. When ready to prepare salad, cut egg in chunks and put in bowl. Add eggplant appetizer and tuna and seasonings. Stir all ingredients lightly. Pull apart onion slices and make into rings; add them to salad. Add 3 tablespoons dressing or more if necessary. Blend into salad and put in refrigerator for about ½ hour. Serve on bed of lettuce. Makes 2 servings.

Phyllis J. Kowal
Southfield, MI

Cauliflower Salad

Preparation time: 30 minutes

½ small cauliflower, cut
and sliced ¼ inch thick
1 carrot, cut in 2-inch
strips
1 stalk celery

½ green pepper, cut in
2-inch strips
1 jar (2 ounces) pimientos
4 pitted green olives

Marinade:

¾ cup wine vinegar
½ cup olive oil
2 tablespoons sugar

1 teaspoon salt
½ teaspoon oregano
Pepper to taste

Combine all marinade ingredients with ¼ cup water. Bring to a boil, add vegetables and then cook 3–5 minutes. Refrigerate until served. Drain when served. Can stay refrigerated for a week. Makes 3–4 servings.

Annetta Van Hoeve
Kalamazoo, MI

Chicken Salad with a Twist

Preparation time: 30 minutes

6–ounce package
   corkscrew macaroni
3 cups cooked chicken,
   diced
½ cup Italian dressing
½ cup mayonnaise
3 tablespoons lemon juice
1 tablespoon prepared
   mustard

1 medium onion, chopped
¾ cup ripe olive wedges
1 cup diced cucumbers
1 cup diced celery
1 teaspoon pepper
Salt
Lettuce

Cook macaroni following the package directions. Mix cooked chicken and Italian dressing with hot macaroni. Cool. Blend mayonnaise, lemon juice, and mustard and stir in chopped onions, olives, cucumbers, celery and pepper. Add to macaroni mixture. Salt to taste. Mix well. Chill 2 or more hours to blend flavor. Serve in lettuce cups. Makes 4 servings.

Rivka A. Pratt
Seattle, WA

Chinese Shrimp Salad

Preparation time: 20 minutes

½ pound shrimp (fresh, frozen or canned)

4 cups celery, chopped fine (may substitute Napa or Chinese cabbage for celery)

1 small can whole water chestnuts, drained and quartered

½ pound fresh bean sprouts (blanched and cooled)

3 to 4 tablespoons mayonnaise (as desired. Real mayonnaise is better than salad dressing)

¼ to ½ teaspoon curry powder

Lemon juice as desired

Combine all ingredients. May be eaten immediately although it is better refrigerated overnight to blend flavors. Makes 4 servings. This recipe can be used for 2 people by cutting ingredients in half, or may be increased to serve a larger group. Do not use lettuce, since it tends to wilt and take away from the crispness of the salad.

Linda Strunk
Sewickley, PA

Crab Salad Strunk

Preparation time: 15 minutes

1 egg yolk
2 tablespoons white wine vinegar
1 tablespoon Dijon mustard
1 tablespoon chopped scallions
2 garlic cloves, minced
½ teaspoon salt
½ teaspoon freshly ground white pepper
¾ cup salad oil
2 large pieces of leaf lettuce
1 chilled ripe avocado, halved, seeded and peeled

8 ounces fresh or frozen crab meat, thawed
1 sprig parsley, minced
1 chilled tomato, quartered or sliced
1 hard-cooked egg, quartered
4 whole Greek olives, pitted
2 artichoke hearts, marinated and drained, cut in half

Combine egg yolk, vinegar, mustard, scallions, garlic, salt and pepper. Whip together with a whisk 1 minute. Add oil very slowly, beating constantly with whisk, till thick. Chill. Arrange leaf lettuce on two plates. Place ½ avocado on each plate. Combine vinaigrette and crab meat, spoon into avocados. Sprinkle with minced parsley. Decorate each salad with tomato, olives, hard-cooked egg quarters and artichoke heart halves. Serve immediately. Makes 2 servings.

Sherry Runk
San Gabriel, CA

Creamy Cottage Dressing

Preparation time: 5 minutes

1 cup cottage cheese
⅓ cup mayonnaise
3 tablespoons honey
1 tablespoon grated lime rind
2 tablespoons lime juice

Place all ingredients in blender container. Cover. Blend until smooth. Chill. Serve over fruit. Yields 2 cups.

Arlene Anton
Bloomfield Hills, MI

Dutch Cole Slaw

Preparation time: 20 minutes

2 cups shredded cabbage
¼ cup minced green pepper
1 tablespoon minced onion
6 slices bacon
⅓ cup mayonnaise
1 tablespoon vinegar
½ teaspoon salt

Combine cabbage, pepper and onion. Saute bacon until crisp. Drain, saving bacon fat. Break bacon into small pieces; toss with cabbage. Combine 2 tablespoons hot bacon fat, mayonnaise, vinegar and salt and heat. Mix dressing with salad. Serve immediately. Makes 2 servings.

Gretchen Snyder
Elmhurst, NY

Fresh Fruit and Yogurt Salad

Preparation time: 25 minutes

- 3 oranges, peeled, seeded and sliced
- 3 apples, peeled, sliced
- 3 bananas, peeled, sliced
- 1 cup sliced pineapple (if not fresh, use canned, drain)
- 1 cup raisins
- 1 cup nuts (halved or chopped)
- 1 cup sunflower seeds (shelled, unsalted)
- 2 pints plain yogurt
- 1/3 cup honey
- ½ cup brown sugar
- 1 teaspoon vanilla
  Cinnamon, mint leaves

Combine fruits, nuts, sunflower seeds in large bowl. In another bowl, mix yogurt, honey, sugar and vanilla. Add to fruits and nuts mixture. Serve in small dishes or large bowl. Sprinkle with cinnamon and garnish with mint leaves.

Michael Usher
Detroit, MI

Guacamole Salad

Preparation time: 20 minutes

- 3 ripe avocados
- 1 whole tomato, chopped
- ¼ cup finely chopped onion
- ¼ cup sunflower seeds
- ¼ cup taco sauce (or to taste)
  Lettuce
- 1 bag of favorite tortilla chips

Peel avocados and remove seeds. Place in bowl and mash. Then add tomatoes, onion, sunflower seeds, and taco sauce. Mix well, and serve on a bed of shredded lettuce. Place chips around Guacamole and serve. Makes 7–8 servings.

Elaine R. Schultz
Birmingham, MI

Hot German Potato Salad

Preparation time: 1 hour

6 medium-size potatoes	¾ cup water
6 strips bacon, cut in thin strips	¼ cup cider vinegar
	½ cup dark brown sugar
4 whole green onions, cut in thin slices	½ teaspoon salt
	Dash pepper
3 tablespoons flour	

Cook potatoes in their jackets in boiling, salted water in a covered saucepan until tender. Peel and slice thin while they are hot. Fry bacon in skillet till crisp. Turn skillet to low heat and add the flour and water, stirring to make it like a gravy. Add the vinegar and brown sugar; if too thick add more water, then salt and pepper. Add warm potato and the green onions and stir together with the bacon and the sauce. May be made night before for better taste. Serves 4, plus leftovers are great!

Patty McDowell
Canton, OH

Hot Seafood Salad

Preparation time: 45 minutes

1 cup crab meat
1 cup shrimp
1 green pepper, sliced
1 small onion, chopped
1½ cups finely sliced celery
1 cup mayonnaise

½ teaspoon salt
Dash of pepper
1 teaspoon Worcestershire sauce
Bread crumbs

Mix all ingredients except bread crumbs. Spoon mixture into baking dish and top with bread crumbs. Bake 30 minutes in 350° oven. This amount will serve 3–4 people. To make hot chicken salad, substitute 2 cups diced chicken for seafood.

Margaret A. Preston
Las Vegas, NV

Hot Zucchini Salad

Preparation time: 15–20 minutes

2 tablespoons butter or margarine
¼ cup chopped onions
1 clove garlic, mashed
1 large (or 2 small) zucchini squashes, sliced

1 small can artichoke hearts, drained and quartered
¼ to ⅓ cup prepared Italian dressing
Salt, pepper

In large skillet, heat butter; saute onions and garlic until tender. Add zucchini and cook until zucchini is tender.

(131)

Add artichokes, Italian dressing and salt and pepper to taste. Cover and let steam for 3 minutes. Serve over lettuce and/or fresh spinach. Makes 2 servings.

Ruth Buechley
Jacksonville, AR

Italian Supper Salad

Preparation time: 30 minutes

1 cup broccoli flowerettes, thinly sliced
1 cup cauliflower flowerettes, thinly sliced
½ cup celery, thinly sliced
¼ cup onions, thinly sliced and separated
1 jar (4 ounces) artichoke hearts, undrained
2 tablespoons red wine vinegar
4 black olives

4 green olives
1 teaspoon garlic salt
¼ teaspoon freshly ground pepper
¼ teaspoon oregano
2 slices Provolone cheese, quartered
1 medium tomato, cut into eighths
2 hard-boiled eggs, quartered

Put all ingredients except cheese, tomato and eggs into a bowl and mix well. Marinate for 20 minutes, stirring occasionally. To serve, spoon the marinated vegetables onto two plates and garnish with the cheese, tomato and eggs. Serves 2. You may marinate this overnight, if desired. Serve with bread sticks or garlic bread.

Laura Newcomer
El Cerrito, CA

Mexican Bean Salad

Preparation time: 12 minutes, to mix, 3 hours to chill

- 2 cans (1 pound each) cut green beans
- 2 cans (1 pound each) garbanzo beans
- 2 cans (1 pound each) kidney beans
- 1 container (8 ounces) sour cream
- 1 packet of chili seasoning mix
- ½ pound grated Cheddar cheese
- 2 cans (4 ounces each) sliced olives
- ½–1 cup chopped onion (optional)

Drain beans in colander. Combine sour cream with seasoning mix. In large bowl, combine beans and sour cream mixture. Add grated cheese, sliced olives, onions if desired. Chill for at least 3 hours. Serve on lettuce leaves and garnish with large olives and a dollop of sour cream. Makes about 8 servings.

Bernadine Pogreba
Omaha, NE

Monterey Salad

Preparation time: 15 minutes

- 1 head lettuce
- 2 apples cut in wedges (dip in lemon juice)
- 2 cups green grapes
- ½ cup sliced celery
- 1 cup Swiss cheese cubes

Arrange all in bowl. Serve with dressing below. Makes 4 servings.

Sweet and Sour Dressing:

¼ cup lime juice
¼ cup light corn syrup
½ cup corn oil
1 teaspoon paprika
½ teaspoon celery seed

½ teaspoon salt
¼ teaspoon onion salt
¼ teaspoon dry mustard
⅛ teaspoon white pepper

Shake together—makes 1 cup.

Celia Entwistle
Dallas, TX

Refrigerated Cucumber Pickles

Preparation time: 20 minutes

4 cups sugar
4 cups white vinegar
1⅓ tablespoons turmeric
1⅓ tablespoons mustard
  seed
½ cup salt

1⅓ tablespoons celery seed
4 quarts sliced cucumbers
1–3 sliced onions
1 green pepper, chopped
  (optional)

Heat sugar, vinegar and seasonings to boiling. Arrange sliced cucumbers, onions, green pepper (if desired) in jars. Pour hot liquid over. Cool, then store in refrigerator.

Ida B. Grenier
Livonia, MI

Salad Nicoise

Preparation time: 20–25 minutes

Crisp lettuce leaves
(leaf, romaine or head)
2 tomatoes, peeled and
quartered
½ sweet onion, sliced
½ green pepper, sliced
2 radishes, trimmed and
sliced
2 stalks celery, sliced
diagonally
1 can (about 6 ounces)
tuna packed in water,
drained
4 anchovy fillets

1 hard-cooked egg,
quartered
4 ripe olives, sliced
*½ cup frozen mixed
vegetables cooked in
boiling salted water,
underdone for crispness.
Optional, but a good
way to use up leftover
mixed vegetables
Salt, pepper
Salad Nicoise Dressing
(below)

Wash lettuce well and dry well on paper towels. Divide between two salad bowls or serving plates, lining each completely. Top with quartered tomatoes, onion, pepper, radishes, celery, tuna (in chunks) and chilled mixed vegetables, dividing ingredients evenly between the 2 servings. Garnish with the anchovy fillets, hard-cooked egg quarters, and sliced olives. Pour entire amount of salad dressing on top and serve. Add salt and freshly ground pepper to taste. Makes 2 servings.

Salad Nicoise Dressing:

1 tablespoon lemon juice
(fresh)

3 tablespoons olive oil
1 teaspoon basil

Mix ingredients well and chill. This is enough for 2 salads.

Ann Wyman
Montclair, CA

Salmon Salad

Preparation time: 30 minutes

- 1 tablespoon vinegar
- 2 tablespoons salad oil
- 1 teaspoon prepared mustard
  Salt and pepper to taste
- 1 medium potato
- 1 can (7 ounces) salmon, drained
- 1 shallot, chopped
- 1 teaspoon chopped parsley
- 1 hard-cooked egg, quartered
- 4 stuffed olives, sliced

Blend the vinegar, oil, mustard, salt and pepper. Refrigerate. Scrub the potato well and cook in salted boiling water. Peel, dice and sprinkle with refrigerated dressing. Add the salmon, shallot and parsley and toss lightly. Garnish with egg wedges and olive slices. Makes 2 servings.

Beth Leonard
Columbus, OH

Spinach Salad

Preparation time: 45 minutes

- 1 egg yolk
- 2 tablespoons sugar
- 1½ teaspoons paprika
- 1 tablespoon Worcestershire sauce
- ½ teaspoon salt
- ¼ teaspoon dry mustard
- ¼ teaspoon pepper
- ¾ cup salad oil
- ¼ cup wine vinegar
- ½ pound fresh spinach
- 1 hard-cooked egg
- 3 strips bacon, cooked crisp
- 1 small red onion

(136)

Prepare dressing first: Mix egg yolk and seasonings until smooth. Continue stirring and add oil slowly; add vinegar. Refrigerate dressing at least ½ hour. Meanwhile, wash spinach thoroughly and remove stems. Dry thoroughly, chill. Chop egg, crumble bacon; dice onion. Before serving, sprinkle eggs, bacon and onion on spinach; toss lightly. Add dressing. Serves 2. Enjoy! Dressing will keep for a week in refrigerator.

Jeanette Kater Nejame
North Miami Beach, FL

Tabuli (Mideastern Salad)

Preparation time: 45 minutes

¾ cup fine cracked wheat
bulgar
1 bunch parsley
½ bunch fresh mint
4–5 large ripe tomatoes

½ bunch scallions
Juice of 2–4 lemons
½ cup oil
Salt, pepper, allspice
Lettuce or grape leaves

Wash cracked wheat in hot water; drain and let set 30 to 40 minutes. While wheat is draining, wash all vegetables and pick leaves of parsley and mint off stems; cut up very fine. Cut tomatoes and dice scallions. Put all vegetables into a large bowl over the softened wheat. Add lemon juice, oil, salt, pepper and allspice to suit taste; mix thoroughly. Serve Tabuli with lettuce or grape leaves. Spoon into leaf and enjoy. Makes 4 servings.

Vegetable

Busy people do unique and wonderful things with vegetables, as this chapter proves. Yvonne Flanigan of Plano, Texas made Spinach Stuffed Peppers, which could serve as an appetizer as well as vegetable. Ms. Flanigan, mother of eight children, works with Kelly Services as a temporary receptionist. She is active in community and sports organizations, loves sailing, and is on the Advisory Council of the church to which she and husband David John belong.

Karen Kampfer
Las Vegas, NV

Bamia (Stew of Okra, Meatless, Persian)

Preparation time: 60 minutes

3 tablespoons vegetable oil
1 small brown onion, chopped
1 teaspoon turmeric
½ teaspoon pepper
2 celery ribs, sliced small
½ cup hot water
1 box (10 ounces) frozen, chopped okra
1 can (6 ounces) tomato paste
1 medium tomato, chopped
½ cup lemon juice
1 cup fresh parsley, chopped
½ green pepper, chopped
4 medium fresh mushrooms, chopped
1 teaspoon mint flakes
Salt to taste

Put oil in medium-size saucepan; add chopped onion, turmeric, and pepper. Saute onion over low heat until limp. Add sliced celery, saute. When celery has become limp, add hot water and let it boil. Add okra, cook uncovered for 5 minutes over medium heat. Add tomato paste, chopped tomato, and lemon juice. Cover and simmer for 20 minutes; stir occasionally. Add parsley, green pepper, mushrooms, mint, and salt. Cover and simmer for 20 minutes. (This dish is served over long-grain white rice, which can be prepared at this time.) Makes 2–3 servings.

Patricia Ethridge
New York, NY

*

Bananaed Sweet Potatoes

Preparation time: About 35 minutes

2 *medium sweet potatoes*
1 *tablespoon butter or margarine*
1 *small onion, chopped*
½ *green pepper, cut into thin strips*
¼ *cup raisins*
2 *tablespoons molasses*
1 *tablespoon soy sauce or tamari*
½ *cup orange juice*
1 *teaspoon ginger*
¼ *teaspoon thyme leaves*
¼ *teaspoon basil leaves*
2 *small bananas, cut into wheels*

Wash and peel potatoes. Plunge into pan of boiling water and cook until tender, about 25 minutes. Melt butter in skillet and cook onions and green pepper on low heat until onions are soft and clear, about 3 minutes. Raise heat to medium and add raisins, liquids, ginger and herbs, and stir until blended. Drain potatoes, cut into large chunks, and add to skillet. Lower heat, add bananas, cover, and cook for 5 minutes. Serve potatoes and bananas at once, pouring liquid over them as a sauce. Makes 2 servings.

Doris Keoppel
Foster City, CA

Bean Sprout Delight

Preparation time: 30 minutes

1 *cup raw rice*
¼ *pound bean sprouts*
1 *small whole onion, chopped*
2 *cloves garlic, crushed*
1 *tablespoon margarine*
1 *small zucchini*
6 *slices bacon, fried and crumbled*

Prepare rice as directed on box. Saute bean sprouts, onion, garlic in frying pan with margarine. Shred zucchini and add to frying pan. Saute until done. Add pre-fried bacon bits and rice, stir until heated. Makes 2 servings.

Barbara Ross Thomson
Glenview, IL

Bourbon Spiced Sweet Potatoes

Preparation time: 1 hour

4 sweet potatoes	¼ teaspoon nutmeg
⅓ cup sugar	½ teaspoon cinnamon
½ cup butter	⅓ cup raisins
2 eggs, lightly beaten	¼ cup Bourbon
¼ teaspoon salt	½ cup heavy cream

Scrub the potatoes and bake until tender. Peel and mash into a bowl. Add remaining ingredients and mix well. Turn into a greased casserole and bake until heated through, about 10 minutes. Makes 6–8 servings.

Martha Augustine
Throop, PA

Butternut Squash Casserole

Preparation time: 55 minutes

4 pounds butternut squash, halved and seedy centers removed	½ to 1 teaspoon crushed rosemary
⅓ cup butter or margarine	¼ to ½ teaspoon ground coriander
2 tablespoons cream	Salted pecans, coarsely chopped (optional)
1 tablespoon grated onion	
1 teaspoon salt	

Put squash halves, cut side down, in a large shallow baking pan. Pour in boiling water to a depth of ¼ inch. Bake at 400° for 30–40 minutes, or until squash is tender. Remove from oven; cool squash slightly. Scoop cooked squash from shells into a bowl and beat with an electric beater until smooth. Add the butter or margarine, cream, onion, and a blend of salt, rosemary, and coriander; beat well. Turn mixture into a greased shallow 1½-quart casserole. Spoon chopped nuts around edge to form a border. Set in a 400° oven about 20 minutes, or until thoroughly heated. Makes 6 to 8 servings.

Melba H. King
Charleston, WV

Caraway Beets

Preparation time: 20 minutes

1½ tablespoons butter
1½ tablespoons flour
½ cup beet liquid
⅛ cup tarragon vinegar
1 tablespoon sugar

1 can (1 pound) small whole beets
½ cup sour cream
2 teaspoons caraway seeds

Melt butter, stir in flour and cook until smooth. Gradually add beet liquid and vinegar and cook, stirring until thick and smooth. Add sugar. Put the beets in the sauce and heat through. To serve, pile beets in serving dish, top with sour cream and sprinkle with caraway seeds. Serves 2–3.

Note: To make tarragon vinegar, use ½ teaspoon tarragon to ½ cup white vinegar . . . let set couple days and strain.

Betty Gee
Holt, MI

Glazed Carrots with Herbs

Preparation time: 40 minutes

1 dozen young carrots	½ teaspoon chervil
1 tablespoon butter	¼ teaspoon basil
1 tablespoon honey	½ teaspoon salt
½ teaspoon chopped chives	

Cook carrots in small amount of water (salted) until tender and water has boiled away. Add butter and honey and cook, turning often, until carrots are evenly cooked and well glazed. Sprinkle carrots lightly with chopped chives, chervil, basil and salt. Makes two servings.

Lorraine Lockrem
Omaha, NE

Holiday Cauliflower

Preparation time: 30 minutes

1 large head cauliflower	1 teaspoon salt
1 can (4 ounces) sliced mushrooms, drained	1 cup shredded Swiss cheese (also add a little yellow cheese for color)
½ cup diced green pepper	
¼ cup butter	2 tablespoons chopped pimiento
⅓ cup flour	
2 cups milk	

Break cauliflower into medium-size flowerettes. Cook in boiling water until crisp-tender. Drain well, set aside. In 2-quart saucepan saute mushrooms and pepper in butter. Blend in flour, stir in milk till thick. Add salt, cheese and pimiento. Place half of cauliflower in buttered casserole, cover with ½ sauce, repeat. Bake at 325° for fifteen minutes. Serves 8.

Therese Tutupalli
Stockton, CA

Indian Potato Curry

Preparation time: 25 minutes

1 teaspoon mustard seeds
1 tablespoon lentils
3 tablespoons cashew nuts, chopped
¼ cup salad oil
2 small green chili peppers, quartered

2 medium onions, chopped
1 teaspoon turmeric
2 teaspoons salt
3 large potatoes, cooked in skins, peeled and lightly mashed

In a large saucepan, fry mustard seed, lentils and cashew nuts in oil for 3–4 minutes. Add chili peppers and onions. Cook for 7–10 minutes, stirring every few minutes. Add turmeric and salt, stir well. Add potatoes and stir well until potatoes are covered evenly by turmeric. Remove from stove. Serves 6 as a side dish.

Sylvia Palmer
Santa Cruz, CA

Kelly Green Rice and Peas

Preparation time: 25 minutes

2 tablespoons chopped
   onion
1 stalk celery, cut fine
1 tablespoon margarine
1 cup cooked rice
¼ teaspoon turmeric
¼ teaspoon salt

Dash pepper
1 raw beaten egg
1 tablespoon chopped
   pimiento
1 cup frozen peas
¼ cup chopped peanuts,
   optional

Saute onion and celery in margarine in medium-size frying
pan over medium flame until vegetables are limp but not
brown. Add rice, turmeric, salt and pepper and stir-fry
2 minutes. Add beaten egg, stirring quickly and mixing
thoroughly until rice is slightly dry. Add pimiento and
peas; cook 1 minute. Cover pan and let stand 5 minutes
before serving. Sprinkle with chopped peanuts, if desired.
Serves two as a side dish or one amply for an entire meal.
A hearty vegetable dish with lots of protein from the egg,
peas and peanuts, so it's a meal-in-one for a busy Kelly gal.

Lucy Rodic
Oxnard, CA

Lucy's Delicious Sweet and Sour Cabbage

Preparation time: 1 hour, 15 minutes

½ small cabbage, coarsely chopped
½ teaspoon salt
2 slices bacon, chopped
½ medium onion, chopped
½ cup canned stewed or whole tomatoes

4 ounces canned butter beans
1½ tablespoons flour
2½ teaspoons brown sugar
Dash black pepper, garlic salt, dry mustard

Boil cabbage and salt in a medium pan filled halfway with water for 10–15 minutes or until cabbage is tender. Saute bacon and onion in a separate pan while cabbage is boiling. Drain juice from tomatoes and beans. Mix juice with flour in a small bowl. Pour juice and flour mixture into onion and bacon, mixture. Stir well. Drain water from cabbage and add flour, onion, bacon, and juice mixture and vegetables. Carefully stir and fold to mix thoroughly. Add sugar and remaining seasonings. Cover and cook slowly for one hour. Makes 2 servings.

Pat Chapman McHaney
Doraville, GA

Marinated Potatoes

Preparation time: Approximately 1 hour

¾ cup salad oil
⅓ cup wine or cider vinegar
¾ teaspoon salt
2 teaspoons sugar
¼ teaspoon pepper
¼ teaspoon dry mustard
¼ teaspoon basil, crushed
1 tablespoon finely chopped parsley

2 tablespoons finely chopped onion
1 tablespoon finely chopped pimiento
6–8 new potatoes or 3–4 white Irish potatoes, cooked

Shake all ingredients except potatoes in a jar. Slice potatoes while still warm and place in a bowl. Sprinkle salt and a little sugar to taste. Let stand about 10 minutes before adding marinade. Pour marinade over potatoes. Let stand 1 or 2 hours at room temperature. Serve hot or cold. Tastes even better after marinating in refrigerator several days. Makes 4 servings.

Maryann Zepp
Lansdale, PA

Mustard Glazed Carrots

Preparation time: 15 minutes

1 pound carrots
½ tablespoon butter
½ tablespoon Dijon mustard

2 tablespoons brown sugar
2 tablespoons parsley

Peel carrots and slice lengthwise and cook in salted boiling water until slightly tender. Drain. Heat butter, mustard and brown sugar until syrupy, about 4 minutes. Saute carrots and glaze together. Serve sprinkled with parsley. Serves 4.

Carline L. Cronan
Taunton, ME

New England Corn Fritters

Preparation time: 10 minutes

2 eggs, separated	1 teaspoon salt
2 tablespoons flour	Dash pepper
1 tablespoon sugar	2 cups grated fresh corn

Beat egg yolks, add flour, sugar, salt and pepper. Add corn to mixture, folding in stiffly beaten egg whites. Use lightly greased frying pan (or spray with no-stick vegetable spray), dropping small spoonfuls of mixture. Cook carefully, very slowly, to brown both sides. Makes 4–6 servings.

Susan Moncure
Richmond, VA

Rich Green Beans

Preparation time: 20 minutes

1 pound fresh green beans, cut into bite-size pieces	¾ cup chopped onions
	1 tablespoon sweet Hungarian paprika
2 quarts water	2 tablespoons flour
1 teaspoon salt	1 cup sour cream
4 tablespoons butter	½ teaspoon salt

Cook beans in water and salt, drain. Melt butter in pan; when foam subsides add onions. Cook until translucent. Take off heat and stir in paprika, stirring till onions are coated. With wire whisk, beat the flour into sour cream. Then stir mixture into skillet with onions; add salt. Simmer on low heat until sauce is smooth and creamy. Stir in beans; simmer till heated through. Serves 4.

Yvonne Flanigan
Plano, TX

Spinach Stuffed Peppers

Preparation time: 1 hour 15 minutes

1 bunch spinach or 1 package (10 ounces) frozen, (thawed and drained well)
½ bunch celery
1 large onion
¼ pound sharp Cheddar cheese

3 eggs, beaten well
1 teaspoon salt
¼ cup olive oil (more if desired)
½ to 1 cup bread crumbs (to bind)
6 green peppers

Wash and clean spinach (use stems too). Clean celery and onions. Grind spinach, celery, onion, cheese and mix well. Then beat eggs, add to spinach mixture. Add salt, olive oil and bread crumbs. If too thin add more crumbs. Clean peppers, cut into quarters. Parboil peppers for 2 minutes. Drain. Place on cookie sheet, lightly salt and fill with spinach mixture. Bake 1 hour at 325°. These can be frozen before baking and then removed from freezer as needed. Freeze on cookie sheet and then store in plastic bags to keep from sticking together. These quarters may be cut in half and served as hors d'oeuvres. Makes about 12 servings.

Denise Carper
Castro Valley, CA

Zesty Zucchini

Preparation time: 15 minutes

2 tablespoons oil
  (preferably olive oil)
  Minced onion and garlic
  to taste
2–3 medium fresh
  tomatoes, chopped
  (canned OK)

3 medium zucchini, sliced
  Salt and pepper to taste
½ teaspoon oregano
  Parmesan cheese

Heat oil in pan to lightly cook onion and garlic (until onion is limp, not brown). Add tomatoes and simmer for a few minutes. Add sliced zucchinis, salt, pepper, oregano and a small amount of water. (Zucchini and tomato have their own liquid.) Cook about 8 minutes at medium heat, uncovered, stir occasionally. Just before serving, sprinkle with Parmesan cheese. Serves 2.

Margaret M. Skinner
Carlstadt, NJ

Zucchini Relish

Preparation time: 1 hour, plus overnight

10 cups zucchini, ground	½ teaspoon pepper
4 cups onions, ground	1 tablespoon nutmeg
2 cups green peppers, ground	1 tablespoon mustard
5 tablespoons salt	1 tablespoon turmeric
2½ cups white vinegar	1 tablespoon cornstarch
4½ cups sugar	2 teaspoons celery salt

Mix together the ground zucchini, onions, green pepper, and salt. Let stand overnight. In morning, drain and rinse in cold water and drain again. Put in a large kettle and add remaining ingredients. Bring to a boil and simmer uncovered for 30 minutes. Put into hot jars and seal. Makes about 5 pints.

Desserts

Scrumptious pies, delectible puddings, fabulous fruits—these desserts are dazzlers. They prove that busy people can enjoy the fun things in life! The winner of this group is rich Kentucky Pie, the inspiration of Cloteal Daigre, of Clinton, Mississippi. A private-duty Practical Nurse, Cloteal works on temporary assignments for the Kelly Health Care Division and is also a member of the Home Demonstrators Club. She demonstrates a penchant for cooking like husband Felix, who was a cook in the U.S. Army. Cloteal hasn't said whether or not hubby shares his recipes with her. The two Daigre children might know!

Linda Sadunas
Cupertino, CA

Apple Coconut Torte

Preparation time: 45 minutes

2 eggs
1½ cups sugar
2 large apples, peeled and
    diced fine
1 teaspoon vanilla

1 cup flour
¼ teaspoon salt
½ cup chopped walnuts
½ cup coconut

Beat eggs and sugar, add diced apples and vanilla. Stir in flour, salt, nuts and coconut. Bake in a well greased 6x10 pan in a 325° oven for 25–35 minutes. Serve with whipped cream. Makes 12 servings:

Matilda C. Hanna
Taylors, SC

Apple Omelet

Preparation time: About 35 minutes

3 tablespoons flour
¼ teaspoon baking powder
    Pinch of salt
2 egg whites
3 tablespoons sugar
3 tablespoons milk

2 egg yolks, well beaten
1 tablespoon lemon juice
1 large unpared apple
¼ cup sugar
½ teaspoon cinnamon

Preheat oven to 375°. Sift flour with baking powder and salt. In medium bowl with beater, beat egg whites until foamy. Then beat in 3 tablespoons of sugar until stiff peaks form. Take flour mixture in small bowl, beat in milk and egg yolks until smooth. With rubber scraper fold in egg whites and lemon juice, just until blended. Slowly heat large buttered skillet or griddle (10 inches) with a metal handle. Turn batter into skillet, spread evenly. Core and slice apples. Arrange apple slices evenly on top. Sprinkle with cinnamon and ¼ cup sugar mixture. Bake 10 minutes or until the top looks glazed. Cut into wedges and serve. Makes 4–5 servings. Great for breakfast, dessert, or for sweet appetizers (cut in smaller pieces). Leftovers can be heated for later or sent with lunch. Good hot or cold.

Shirley Koegel
Roanoke, IN

Apple Pudding

Preparation time: 1 hour

½ cup shortening
2 cups sugar
2 eggs
2 cups flour
2 teaspoons soda
½ teaspoon salt

2 teaspoons nutmeg
2 teaspoons cinnamon
4 cups finely cut apples
½ cup chopped nuts
(preferably pecans)

Sauce:

½ cup butter
½ cup cream

½ cup sugar
1 teaspoon vanilla

Cream together shortening and sugar; add eggs. Add dry ingredients (which have been sifted together) alternately with apples. Add nuts. Bake 40 minutes at 350° in 9 by 13 inch greased pan. Serve with Warm Sauce poured over. Makes 12 servings.

Warm Sauce: Bring to a boil all ingredients.

Marilyn Michaelis
Arvada, CO

Applescotch Pie

Preparation time: 1½ hours

5 cups apples (peeled,
  sliced)
1 cup brown sugar
¼ cup water
1 tablespoon lemon juice
¼ cup sifted flour
2 tablespoons granulated
  sugar

1 teaspoon vanilla
¾ teaspoon salt
3 tablespoons butter
Pastry for 2-crust
9-inch pie
Cinnamon
Butter

Combine the apples, brown sugar, water and the lemon juice in a saucepan. Cover; cook slowly until apples are just tender, 7 to 8 minutes. Blend flour, sugar; add to apples. Cook, uncovered, stirring constantly, until the syrup thickens, about 2 minutes. Remove from heat. Add the vanilla, salt, and the butter. Cool to room temperature. Heat oven to 425°. Line 9-inch pan; fill with apple mixture. Sprinkle with cinnamon and dot with butter. Cover with top crust; slit for steam to escape. Bake 40 to 45 minutes. Makes one 9-inch pie.

Lynnette Bauman
Blairsville, PA

Baked Apples Linby

Preparation time: 50 minutes

½ teaspoon lemon juice
¼ cup water
2 large tart apples
¼ cup butter
2 tablespoons sugar
¼ teaspoon nutmeg

¼ teaspoon ginger
½ teaspoon cinnamon
¼ cup black walnuts,
  chopped
1 cup miniature
  marshmallows

Combine lemon juice and water in a small bowl. Wash, peel and core apples; cut in half. Dip apple halves into lemon water, set aside. Preheat oven to 350°. Use 1 tablespoon butter to grease small baking dish (large enough to hold apples). Cream remaining butter (3 tablespoons), sugar, nutmeg, ginger, and cinnamon. Mix in walnuts and marshmallows. Place 2 apple halves in baking dish. Mound the marshmallow mixture into the well of each apple. Cover with remaining apple halves. Bake for 35 minutes. Makes 2 servings.

Anne Pratley
Holden, MA

Best Ever Lemon Sherbet

Preparation time: 30 minutes

Juice and rind of 1 lemon	*1 cup sugar*
	1 cup milk
Juice and rind of 1 orange	*1 cup heavy cream, whipped stiff*

Combine juice and grated rind of lemon and orange with sugar, and allow to stand overnight in a covered bowl; this is most important. In the morning, add the milk slowly, and the cream whipped stiff. Pour into refrigerator tray and freeze, stirring once while freezing. Makes eight servings but you will want to make whole recipe as it is. Positively delicious and keeps well.

Patsy Crittenden
Detroit, MI

Blueberry Slump

Preparation time: 25 minutes

- 2 cups fresh or frozen blueberries
- 1 cup water
- ½ cup sugar
- ¾ cup all purpose flour
- ¼ cup sugar
- ½ teaspoon baking soda
- ¼ teaspoon salt
- ½ cup butter
- 2 tablespoons buttermilk

In a 3-quart sauce pan mix blueberries, water, and the ½ cup sugar. Bring to boiling. Cover, reduce heat and simmer 5 minutes. Combine flour, the ¼ cup sugar, soda and salt. Cut butter into flour mixture till mixture resembles coarse crumbs. Stir in buttermilk just till flour is moistened. Drop batter by tablespoons atop bubbling blueberries mixture, making six dumplings. Cover pan tightly; simmer 15 minutes (don't lift cover). Makes 6 servings.

Elaine Eisenberg
Houston, TX

Cheese Torte

Preparation time: 55 minutes

- 2 tablespoons butter
- 1 pint cottage cheese
- 2 tablespoons sour cream
- 2 eggs
- Salt to taste
- 1 prepared pie shell

Mix butter, cottage cheese, sour cream, eggs and salt. Pour into pie shell. Start in cold oven, set for 300°. Bake about 45 minutes. Can serve with fruit as dessert. Excellent after bridge or cards for late snack.

Suzanne Larkin
Stamford, CT

Chocolate Dessert

Preparation time: 1 hour

1 package (6 ounces) semi-sweet chocolate morsels	*¾ cup sugar*
	2 eggs
	1½ teaspoons vanilla
½ cup butter	*1 cup wheat germ*

Melt chocolate morsels with butter over double boiler. Combine with sugar, eggs, vanilla, and wheat germ. Pour into deep, 9-inch round baking dish. Bake at 350° for 35-45 minutes. A healthy and delicious dessert for two.

Jeanine Van Herwaarden
Dexter, OR

Chocolate Oatmeal Cookies

Preparation time: 10 minutes

2 cups sugar	*3 cups oatmeal (quick-cooking)*
½ cup milk	
½ cup margarine	*1 cup walnuts (optional) chopped*
5 tablespoons cocoa	
1 teaspoon vanilla	

Combine sugar, milk and margarine in saucepan. Bring to boil. Boil exactly 1½ minutes. Remove from heat. Add cocoa, vanilla. Stir. Add oatmeal and nuts. Drop by tablespoons onto waxed paper. Will be firm and ready to eat in 5 or 10 minutes. Makes 50-60 cookies.

Julia J. Codilis
Glenview, IL

Chocolate-orange Mousse

Preparation time: 20 minutes, plus chilling time

½ teaspoon grated orange
rind
2 tablespoons light brown
sugar
1 egg yolk
1 whole egg

3 squares semi-sweet
chocolate, melted and
cooled
1½ tablespoons orange juice
¼ cup heavy cream

Combine orange rind, sugar, egg yolk and egg in blender.
Blend until light and foamy. Add chocolate, orange juice
and cream. Whirl until well blended. Pour into 2 dessert
dishes and chill for 1 hour or until set. Serves 2.

A. Marie Shores
St. Louis, MO

Choco-rum-strata Pie

Preparation time: Approximately 1 hour

1 cup milk
2 egg yolks
¼ cup sugar
½ tablespoon cornstarch
½ envelope (2 teaspoons)
unflavored gelatin
⅛ cup cold water
½ cup semi-sweet
chocolate chips
1 9-inch baked pie shell
½ teaspoon rum flavoring
or ½ jigger rum

2 egg whites
¼ cup sugar to add to egg
whites
1 cup whipping cream,
whipped
2 tablespoons powdered
sugar for sweetening
cream
Chocolate decorettes or
curls as needed

Scald milk in a double boiler. Beat egg yolks and add ¼ cup sugar and cornstarch, stirring to blend. Add this to scalded milk. Cook, stirring as necessary until it coats a spoon. Soak gelatin in ⅛ cup water and set aside. Pour ½ cup hot custard over chocolate chips, blending until smooth, and then spooning into pie shell. Soaked gelatin is added to remaining custard, along with the rum, and is stirred until dissolved. Chill until slightly thickened. Beat egg whites until stiff, gradually adding ¼ cup sugar. The custard is spooned with a folding motion into the egg whites. This is spooned over the chocolate layer in the pie shell. This is then topped with sweetened whipped cream and chocolate decorettes and chilled. Makes 6-8 servings.

Lynn Griffin
Troy, MI

Chocolate Souffle

Preparation time: 1 hour

2 squares unsweetened chocolate	1 teaspoon vanilla
3 tablespoons butter	2 tablespoons rum
2 tablespoons flour	4 egg yolks
¼ teaspoon salt	4 egg whites, stiffly beaten
1 cup milk	½ pint whipping cream
½ cup sugar	

Preheat oven to 350°. Butter 2-quart souffle dish. Sprinkle sides with granulated sugar. Melt chocolate and butter together. Blend in flour and salt until smooth. Gradually add milk, sugar and vanilla, and cook, stirring constantly, until thick and smooth. Remove from heat and cool slightly. Stir in rum. Add egg yolks and beat well. Fold in the beaten egg whites and pour into a souffle dish. Set in a pan of hot water and bake in oven at 350° for 45 minutes. Serve warm with whipped cream passed separately. Serves two.

Lucille I. Maya
El Paso, TX

Cottage Cheese Pie

Preparation time: 1½ hours

16 ounces cream cottage cheese
3 eggs
1 cup sugar
1¼ cups melted butter
⅓ cup lemon juice

1 teaspoon vanilla
¼ cup confectioners' sugar
1 can (no. 2) sliced peaches (can use strawberries, pineapple, cherries)

Crust:

1 package of honey graham crackers (1 box 16 ounces—contains 3 individual packages)

¼ cup melted butter or margarine
¼ cup confectioners' sugar

Cream in blender cottage cheese with eggs, remove from blender, and with wood spoon mix in sugar, melted butter, lemon juice, vanilla, and confectioners' sugar. Put aside or put in refrigerator while crust is being prepared. Also drain all juice from peaches; put in separate bowl. Start preparing pie crust by crushing crackers in pie dish with edge of rolling pin, mixing butter, and confectioners' sugar into crushed crumbs and pressing with fork all around pie dish sides and bottom, forming a smooth shell. Pour in filling. Bake for approximately 45 minutes at 350°. Remove from oven, place on rack, and after it has cooled for 20 minutes, arrange peaches all around pie in a circular arrangement, starting with center of pie. Chill in refrigerator until ready to serve. Serves 6.

Sharon F. Greene
Phoenix, AZ

French Mint Pie

Preparation time: About 30 minutes

1 cup powdered sugar	2 unbeaten eggs
1 stick of butter or margarine	9 drops of the essence of peppermint
2 squares unsweetened chocolate	1 8-inch baked graham cracker pie shell

Cream together 1 cup powdered sugar and one stick of butter or margarine. Melt 2 squares unsweetened chocolate in a small pan and allow to cool before adding to sugar. Take 2 unbeaten eggs (use a small mixing bowl) add one at a time and beat thoroughly—preferably with an electric beater. Add the 9 drops of essence of peppermint. Pour into shell and chill at least six hours or overnight. I have yet to find a man who doesn't like it—try it once and you will make it again. The pie is very rich so serve small servings and place a half pecan on each serving, if you wish.

Joy C. Wooten
Tallahassee, FL

Fresh Banana-rhubarb Pie

Preparation time: 1 hour

Pastry for 2-crust pie
1 pound fresh rhubarb, sliced (3 cups)
3 medium ripe bananas, peeled and sliced (3 cups)
1 cup sugar
¼ cup freshly squeezed orange juice
3 tablespoons flour
¼ teaspoon salt
¼ teaspoon ground cinnamon
¼ teaspoon ground nutmeg
1 tablespoon butter or margarine

Prepare pastry. Roll out half the pastry to a 12-inch circle; line 9-inch pie plate. In large bowl, combine rhubarb, bananas, sugar, orange juice, flour, salt, cinnamon and nutmeg; turn into the pastry-lined pie plate. Dot with butter. Roll remaining pastry for top crust; cut vents to allow steam to escape. Place over filling; seal; flute. Bake at 450° for 15 minutes. Reduce heat at 350° and bake 30 minutes longer or until pie is golden brown. Cool completely.

Michelle L. Gabriel
San Antonio, TX

Frosted Oranges in the Snow

Preparation time: 25 minutes, plus freezing time

1 cup water	¼ cup flaked coconut
⅓ cup sugar	⅛ cup or 2 tablespoons of
Grated rind and juice of	your favorite fruit-
½ lemon	flavored liqueur
¼ cup of your favorite	1 egg white, beaten until
fruit-flavored liqueur	foamy
1 egg white, stiffly beaten	Granulated sugar
2 large oranges	

In a saucepan, combine water and sugar. Bring mixture to a boil and boil for 5 minutes. Remove from heat and stir in lemon rind and juice and liqueur. Pour mixture into a freezer container and freeze until mushy. Pour mixture into a bowl and freeze until hard. With a sharp knife, slice ⅓ off top of each orange. With knife, cut out pulp of orange, leaving shell whole. Remove membrane from pulp, cut into sections, and place in a bowl. Fold in coconut and liqueur. Chill. Brush outside of orange shell and top of orange with slightly beaten egg white. Dip into granulated sugar until well coated. Let dry at room temperature until crusty. Fold orange and coconut mixture into frozen mixture, which has been beaten smooth. When ready to serve, fill orange shell with frozen mixture. Replace top of orange and serve garnished with fresh mint sprigs, if desired. Serve at once. Makes 2 servings.

Frances E. (Sue) Miller
Fullerton, CA

Frosted Strawberry Squares

Preparation time: 1 hour

½ cup melted butter
¼ cup brown sugar
(packed)
½ cup finely chopped nuts
1 cup flour
1 cup heavy cream
(whipping)

2 egg whites
1 cup sugar
2 packages (10 ounces
each) frozen
strawberries, partially
thawed
2 teaspoons lemon juice

Mix first four ingredients, spread evenly in glass pan 9x13 inches. Bake in 350° oven for about 20 minutes or until lightly browned, stirring occasionally. Cool. Whip cream and place in refrigerator. Beat egg whites until soft peaks form, add sugar 1 tablespoon at a time and beat until all sugar is used and egg whites form stiff peaks. Add strawberries a small amount at a time, beating constantly; beat for 10 minutes longer. Fold in whipped cream and lemon juice. Sprinkle about ⅔ of the crumbs in bottom of 9x13-inch pan. Spread filling over crumbs, spread remaining crumbs over top and press down gently. Cover with plastic wrap and place in freezer. Freeze for at least 6 hours or overnight. Let it sit out ½ hour before serving. Makes 16 servings.

Vera Kover
Beaverton, OR

Fruit Cobbler

Preparation time: 1 hour, 15 minutes

1½ cups sugar
2 tablespoons butter
½ cup milk
1 cup flour
2 teaspoons baking
    powder

Pinch of salt
3 boxes youngberries or
    other fruit
½ cup water or juice

Mix ½ cup sugar, butter, milk, flour, baking powder, salt. Pour into greased pan or 2-quart casserole. Cover with youngberries or other fruit. Mix 1 cup sugar in ½ cup boiling water or juice. Pour over top of batter. Bake in 350° oven for 1 hour. Can be served warm or cold with milk, or whipped topping. Makes 12 servings.

If canned fruit is used, reserve the juice to mix with the sugar to pour over top of batter.

Sophia G. Paspalas
St. Louis, MO

Galatobouriko Rolls (Greek Custard Rolls)

Preparation time: 1½ hours

4 slightly beaten eggs
½ cup farina (enriched
    farina)
1 cup sugar
3 cups milk
1 tablespoon butter
1 teaspoon vanilla

1 pound phyllo (strudel
    leaves)
½ pound melted butter
3 cups sugar
2 cups water
1 slice lemon
1 teaspoon vanilla

Combine eggs, farina and sugar; heat milk and slowly add to egg mixture, stirring constantly. Cook over low flame, stirring until mixture is thick, about one-half hour. Add butter and vanilla. Cool for several hours. Take individual sheets of pastry and cut 6 inches wide, keeping the full length of the phyllo. Brush generously with melted butter. Place one tablespoon of custard mixture at the bottom of phyllo and roll up, tucking in sides. Brush top with butter and bake at 350° for 30 minutes until golden brown. While still warm from the oven, top with a cool syrup: boil sugar and water until sugar is dissolved. Reduce heat, add lemon and vanilla and simmer 20 minutes. These rolls may be frozen before baking. Remove from freezer and bake; then pour cool syrup over top. (Strudel leaves may be purchased at an import grocery store.) Makes approximately 45 rolls.

Jean Ponce Paradiso
Jacksonville, FL

Glorified Lemon Pie

Preparation time: 40 minutes

2 cups milk
1¼ cups sugar
8 tablespoons cornstarch
   Dash salt
1 egg plus 1 egg yolk
2 tablespoons lemon juice
   or more to suit your
   taste

1 tablespoon lemon peel
¼ teaspoon vanilla
1 9-inch pie shell

Heat milk in double boiler until hot, do not boil. Mix sugar, cornstarch and salt until smooth. Add the hot milk, slowly mix for one minute until well blended and smooth. Add eggs, lemon juice and peel, mix well. Pour this mixture back into double boiler, heat until mixture begins to coat the side of pan, then stir constantly until thick; this prevents lumping. Gently fold in vanilla. Set aside to cool to room temperature. After mixture has cooled pour into a prepared crust, also good in graham cracker crust. This may be served in custard cups for a super lemon custard. Above makes 1 pie. Double for two.

Deborah Jordan
Tacoma, WA

The Honorary Kelly Cheesecake or The Emerald Isle Chocolate Dream Cake

Preparation time: 1½ hours plus chilling time

⅓ cup butter
⅓ plus ½ cup honey
5 eggs
1¼ cups plus 1 tablespoon flour
2 tablespoons cocoa
20 ounces cream cheese

3 tablespoons creme de cacao
6 tablespoons creme de menthe (green)
⅔ cup sour cream
6–8 ounces sweet chocolate

Cream butter and ⅓ cup honey. Add 1 egg. Mix in 1¼ cups flour and cocoa. Press onto sides and bottom of a 9-inch springform pan. Bake at 350° for 5 minutes (May need to "push" sides of crust 1¼ inches high around sides of pan after baking). Cream 1 tablespoon flour, cream cheese and ½ cup honey. Beat in the 4 eggs, one at a time. Stir in the liqueurs. Bake at 350° for 45 minutes. Cool 10 minutes. Melt chocolate in top of double boiler and mix well with sour cream (a wire whisk works well). Spread cheesecake with topping. Chill well; overnight is best. Makes 12 servings.

Susan Moncure
Richmond, VA

Hungarian Plum Delight

Preparation time: 50 minutes

½ cup butter
½ cup sugar
2 eggs
1 cup sifted enriched
  flour
1 teaspoon baking powder
½ teaspoon salt

2 teaspoons cinnamon
1 tablespoon lemon juice
10 fresh or canned plum
   halves, or 2 cups
   chopped cranberries
½ cup brown sugar
Pinch cardamom

Cream butter, add sugar (white) and cream until light and fluffy. Add eggs one at a time and beat well. Add flour which has been sifted with baking powder, salt and 1 teaspoon cinnamon. Add lemon juice. Pour into well greased pan (11x6x2 inches). Press plum halves into batter (or spread cranberries lightly). Sprinkle mixture of brown sugar, 1 teaspoon cinnamon and cardamom onto batter and fruit. Bake at 400° for 30 minutes. Makes about 10 servings.

Angela A. Yankelitis
Scranton, PA

Italian Ricotta Cream Dessert

Preparation time: 15 minutes, plus chilling time

1½ cups whole milk ricotta cheese

1 tablespoon milk

2 tablespoons sugar (more or less to taste)

½ teaspoon vanilla

⅛ teaspoon orange rind, grated from orange

2 tablespoons chopped sweet chocolate

1 tablespoon chopped almonds

2 slices sponge or pound cake, cut in small cubes

2 tablespoons whiskey, rum or other liquor

4 maraschino cherries (optional)

Put ricotta cheese and milk in small deep bowl and beat with electric mixer or wooden spoon until no lumps remain and cheese is creamy smooth. Add sugar and stir in well. Add vanilla, orange rind, chocolate and almonds. Blend gently. Set out four dishes of dessert size, but with a depth of about 2 inches. Put one fourth of cake cubes into each dish and sprinkle ½ tablespoon of liquor on each. Then spoon on ricotta cream, covering cake cubes smoothly, decorate with cherries if desired. Cover each dish with plastic wrap and refrigerate for 1 or more hours before serving. Makes 4 servings.

Cloteal Daigre
Clinton, MS

Kentucky Pie

Preparation time: 40 minutes

2 cups buttermilk
7 egg yolks
1 cup pecans, chopped
2 tablespoons flour
2 cups sugar
1 cup raisins
2 tablespoons butter

1 teaspoon spice (cloves
   and cinnamon)
   Small pinch salt
2 8-inch baked pie shells
7 egg whites
7 tablespoons sugar
1 teaspoon vanilla extract

Mix the first 9 ingredients well and place in double boiler.
Boil over medium heat until thickened. Pour into baked
pie shells. In a mixing bowl place the egg whites. Beat
until light and fluffy. Beat in seven tablespoons sugar and
1 teaspoon vanilla flavoring. Place in oven (350°) and
brown. Remove from oven, and cool. Serves 16.

Jack H. Seelye
Oakbrook, IL

Kiwi Kirsch Sherbet

Preparation time: 12 minutes, plus freezing time

4 kiwis
6 tablespoons kirsch
½ cup sugar
¼ cup light corn syrup
   Pinch of salt

1 egg white
2 cups rich cold milk, or
   1 cup light cream plus
   1 cup milk

Mash kiwis (approximately 2 cups puree). Blend in kirsch
alternately with sugar and syrup. Add salt and mix thor-

oughly. Fold in stiffly beaten egg white. Stir in milk slowly. Turn mixture into refrigerator tray and freeze. Makes 8 servings.

Marian E. Hite
Swedesboro, NJ

Kugel

Preparation time: 1 hour, 30 minutes

½ pound egg noodles	12 ounces cottage cheese
4 eggs	¼ pound butter, melted
¾ cup sugar	¼ cup raisins
½ teaspoon vanilla	Cinnamon for top
½ pound sour cream	

Cook noodles until soft. Drain. Mix eggs and ½ cup sugar (save ¼ cup sugar). Beat eggs, sugar and add vanilla. Blend in sour cream and cottage cheese. Add butter. Fold in noodles and raisins. Pour mixture into 13x9-inch pan and sprinkle top with remaining sugar and cinnamon. Bake at 350° for one hour and fifteen minutes. Serves 10-15 people.

Norene Wessel
Clarksville, IN

Lemon Layer Pie

Preparation time: 1 hour

2 tablespoons unflavored
  gelatin
⅓ cup fresh lemon juice
3 eggs, beaten
1¼ cups sugar
1½ tablespoons butter
  Grated peel of 1 lemon

1 cup whipping cream,
  whipped
2 sticks instant pie crust
  mix
  Additional grated lemon
  peel for garnish, if
  desired

Soften gelatin in lemon juice. Mix with eggs, sugar, butter
and peel in saucepan. Cook over low heat, stirring until
mixture thickens. Remove from heat; cover, chill until mixture mounds slightly when dropped from spoon. Heat
oven to 475°. Mix pastry as directed on package. Make
9-inch pie shell with half the dough. Bake 8 to 10 minutes.
Cool. Roll rest of dough into two 6-inch rounds; place on
baking sheet, prick, bake 8 to 10 minutes. Cool. Fold half
of whipped cream into filling. Spread ⅓ of filling in pie
shell; top with baked round, more filling, last baked round
and balance of filling. Garnish with balance of whipped
cream, in dollops around the pie. Sprinkle additional
lemon peel on dollops. Chill at least one hour.

Evelynne C. Carpentier
Rockville, MD

Malt Shop Pie

Preparation time: 30 minutes

1 pint vanilla ice cream
½ cup crushed malted milk balls
1 tablespoon milk
1 9-inch graham cracker crumb crust
3 tablespoons instant chocolate-flavored malted milk powder
3 tablespoons marshmallow topping
1 tablespoon milk
1 cup whipping cream
Crushed malted milk balls for topping

In a chilled medium bowl stir ice cream to soften; blend in the ½ cup crushed malted milk balls and the first 1 tablespoon milk. Spread in prepared crust; freeze while preparing top layer. In medium bowl blend malted milk powder, marshmallow topping, and remaining milk. Add whipping cream; whip until soft peaks form. Spread mixture over layer in crust. Freeze until firm, several hours or overnight. Sprinkle with crushed malted milk balls. Makes 6 servings.

Ida B. Grenier
Livonia, MI

Orange Broiled Bananas with Ice Cream

Preparation time: 10 minutes

1 large banana, peeled
1 tablespoon butter, melted
¼ cup brown sugar, firmly packed
¼ cup orange juice
1 teaspoon grated orange peel
1 teaspoon chopped candied ginger
1 cup (2 scoops) vanilla ice cream

(174)

Cut the banana in half lengthwise and crosswise, to make 4 pieces. Arrange pieces in a baking dish in a single layer. Pour melted butter over. Mix the sugar, orange juice, orange peel and candied ginger and pour over the bananas. Broil 8 inches from source of heat for 5 minutes or until bananas are glazed. Serve hot, topped with scoop of ice cream. Spoon some of the sauce over the ice cream. Two servings. Double recipe to serve four.

Cathy Banas
Fresno, CA

Osgood Pie

Preparation time: 1 hour

¾ cup raisins	3 eggs, separated
¼ cup butter	2 teaspoons vinegar
1½ cups sugar	½ cup chopped nuts
1 teaspoon cinnamon	9–inch unbaked pastry
½ teaspoon nutmeg	shell

Rinse, drain and chop raisins. Cream butter, sugar, and spices well. Blend in beaten egg yolks and vinegar. Stir in raisins and nuts. Fold in beaten egg whites. Bake in unbaked pastry shell at 425° for 10 minutes, then 325° for 30 minutes. Test with a silver knife for doneness. Very rich—very good! Makes 6 servings.

Ida Rena Strouse
Fort Wayne, IN

Peach Cobbler

Preparation time: 50 minutes

1 stick margarine
1 cup flour
1 cup sugar
1½ teaspoons baking
   powder
   Pinch of salt
¾ cup milk
½ cup sugar

1 teaspoon nutmeg
3 cups fruit: our favorite
   is peach; but apple
   or blackberries are
   scrumptious too! Just
   alter sugar and spice
   (cinnamon for apple)
   accordingly.

Set oven at 350°, place the stick of margarine in a 12x9x2-inch glass baking dish and into the oven to melt, while you are mixing other ingredients. Into small mixing bowl mix flour, sugar, baking powder, salt, and milk (very thin mixture) and pour over melted margarine. Pour fruit over batter (either frozen or fresh fruit), sweeten and spice, and bake. Use about ½ cup sugar and scant teaspoonful of nutmeg, mixed together, then sprinkle over the peaches. Bake about 20-25 minutes at 350°. Serve warm with cream or ice cream. Yummy! This is so quick and easy to make and can be ready by the time the rest of the meal is—no crust to roll! Serves about 10, if they don't come back for seconds. . . .

Arlene M. Hirsch
Winnipeg, Canada

Peach Kuchen

Preparation time: 1 hour

2 pounds (about 6) ripe
peaches, peeled and
sliced, and 2 tablespoons
lemon juice, OR 2 cans
(14 ounces each) sliced
peaches
1½ cups all-purpose flour
¾ cup sugar
2 teaspoons baking
powder
½ teaspoon salt
2 eggs

2 tablespoons milk
1½ tablespoons grated
lemon rind
¼ cup butter, melted
½ teaspoon cinnamon
1 egg yolk
3 tablespoons whipping
cream
Sweetened, whipped
cream or vanilla ice
cream

If using fresh peaches, sprinkle with lemon juice to prevent darkening; set aside. Sift flour, ½ cup sugar, baking
powder and salt together. In large mixing bowl, beat eggs
with milk and lemon rind. Add flour mixture and butter,
mixing with fork until smooth, about 1 minute. *Do not
overmix.* Turn batter into a greased 9-inch layer cake pan;
spread evenly over bottom. (At this point, kuchen may be
refrigerated several hours or until about a half an hour
before baking.) Drain peach slices; arrange on batter
around edge of pan; fill in center with five peach slices.
Mix remaining ¼ cup sugar and cinnamon together. Sprinkle mixture evenly over peach slices. Bake in oven for
25-35 minutes at 350°. Remove kuchen from oven. With a
fork beat egg yolk with cream. Pour over peaches. Bake
10 minutes longer. Cool for 10 minutes on a wire rack.
Serve kuchen warm cut into wedges with sweetened
whipped cream or vanilla ice cream. Yields 8-10 servings.

Bonnie Crawford
Memphis, TN

Peach Tarts

Preparation time: 1½ hours plus chilling time for dough

Pastry:

½ cup plus 2 tablespoons
    unbleached flour
3 tablespoons cold butter,
    cut into bits

1 tablespoon vegetable oil
1½ teaspoons sugar
1½ tablespoons ice water

Filling:

2 fresh peaches, peeled
    and sliced
1 egg
1 tablespoon flour

⅔ cup granulated sugar
⅙ cup melted butter
¼ teaspoon almond extract
¼ teaspoon vanilla extract

In a large bowl combine flour, butter, oil, and sugar. Blend the ingredients until they are combined and add the ice water. Toss the mixture until the water is incorporated, and form the dough into a ball. Knead the dough lightly with the heel of the hand against a smooth surface a few seconds to distribute the fat evenly, and reform it into a ball. Dust the dough with flour, wrap it in waxed paper, and chill it for 1 hour. Roll out the dough into 2 circles and line the bottoms of two 4-inch tart pans. Arrange the peaches in the pans. Combine the remaining ingredients and blend well. Pour over peaches. Bake for 15 minutes at 400 degrees, reduce heat, and bake 50 minutes longer. Serve hot, garnished with French vanilla ice cream. Makes 4 servings.

Jeanne L. Austin
Hialeah, FL

Peanut Butter Apple Crisp

Preparation time: 1 hour

6 tart, firm apples	2 tablespoons peanut butter
1 teaspoon lemon juice	
½ cup flour (whole wheat preferred)	2 tablespoons butter or margarine
½ cup brown sugar	Pinch of salt

Peel, core and slice apples thinly. Arrange in greased shallow baking dish, about 7x11 inches. Sprinkle with lemon juice. Mix flour, sugar and salt in bowl. Cut in peanut butter and butter until mixture is crumbly. Spread over apples. Bake in moderate oven (375°) about 50 minutes or until apples are tender. If you have ice cream or whipped cream handy, put some on each serving. Garnish with thin slices of red-skinned apple if you really want to be fancy! Serves 6.

Shell Simmers
South Pasadena, CA

Pear Crunch

Preparation time: 30 minutes

2 medium-size pears, cut into chunks	½ teaspoon cinnamon
1 teaspoon honey	10–12 pecan halves, chopped coarsely
⅔ cup granola or granola-type cereal	3 tablespoons whole wheat flour
1 tablespoon brown sugar	2 tablespoons butter

Spray 2 10-ounce ramekins with no-stick vegetable spray. Put 1 pear, cut into chunks, in each. Drizzle each with

½ teaspoon honey. In small bowl combine granola, brown sugar, cinnamon, pecans and flour. Cut in butter. Sprinkle mixture over the pears. Bake at 325°, 20-25 minutes. Serve warm, plain or with whipped cream or ice cream. Makes 2 servings.

Laina Dipzinski
Sterling Hts., MI

Pineapple Squares

Preparation time: 50 minutes

Pastry:

1 cup flour
½ cup margarine

3 tablespoons powdered sugar

Filling:

2 eggs
1 cup sugar
¼ cup flour
½ teaspoon baking powder
¼ teaspoon salt

1 teaspoon vanilla
¾ cup chopped nuts
¾ cup coconut
1 can (8 ounces) crushed pineapple

With hands, mix flour, sugar and margarine until crumbly like pie crust. Spread thin in lightly greased 8x8-inch pan. Bake 20 minutes at 350°. Beat eggs slightly. Stir rest of filling ingredients into the eggs and spread on pastry. Return to the oven and bake 20-30 more minutes. Cool and cut into squares. Makes 16 pieces.

Jeanette Kral
Omaha, NE

Plum Dumplings

Preparation time: 30 minutes

2 cups flour
1 teaspoon salt
2 eggs
½ cup milk

½ stick margarine
6–12 blue plums
1–2 tablespoons sugar

Mix flour and salt together, make a well and add the eggs, milk and softened margarine. Stir well and form into a ball. If mixture is very sticky then add a little more flour. Roll out on a floured board and cut into 4-inch squares. Wash plums. Cut each plum half open and remove the seed. Put ¼-½ teaspoon sugar inside each plum. Wrap one square of dough around each plum and secure the edges. Drop into boiling water and cook until done (approximately 10-15 minutes). Serve with melted butter, cinnamon and sugar. They also may be served topped with cottage cheese as a main dish. Makes 6-12 dumplings.

Anita Pine
San Gabriel, CA

Poppy Seed Chiffon Pie

Preparation time: 1½ hours

Pie Crust:

½ cup graham crackers, crushed (7 small squares)

½ cup breadcrumbs
½ cup walnuts, chopped
¼ cup margarine, melted

Filling:

1½ envelopes unflavored
  gelatin
3 tablespoons cornstarch
¼ cup sugar
¼ cup poppy seeds
2 cups whole milk

4 egg yolks, well beaten
1 teaspoon Cointreau
  (or vanilla)
4 egg whites
⅛ cup sugar

Mix gelatin, cornstarch, sugar, and poppy seeds in saucepan. Stir in milk and heat over medium heat, constantly stirring, until thickened and bubbly 10 minutes. Gradually pour half of this mixture into beaten yolks, at the same time quickly mixing. Then pour back to saucepan and cook 3 minutes longer. Remove from heat, add flavoring, cover and cool in icebox until partially set—about 45 minutes. Beat egg whites until soft peaks form. Gradually beat in ⅛ cup sugar until stiff peaks. Fold cooled mix into egg whites. Pour into baked pie shell. Chill well or overnight.

Karin Sheardown
Anchorage, AK

Rhubarb Custard Pastry Pie

Preparation time: 55 minutes

Crust:

½ cup or 1 stick softened
  butter (margarine will
  not give same flavor)
1 egg
1 teaspoon baking powder

¼ cup sugar
1¼ cups flour
3 cups fresh rhubarb,
  diced (if frozen is used,
  drain after dicing)

Custard topping:

2 eggs
1 teaspoon nutmeg
3 tablespoons flour
1 cup brown sugar
   (increase sugar if
   rhubarb is exceptionally
   tart)

Mix first five ingredients. Pat dough into 9-inch pie pan or springform with fingers. Put diced rhubarb on pastry base. Beat eggs and add rest of ingredients. Pour custard mixture over the rhubarb. Bake at 350° for 45 minutes or until center looks slightly crusty. Can be enjoyed warm but best chilled. Whipped cream makes a beautiful topping but not necessary. Makes 6-8 servings.

Mrs. Mary Lee Leigh
Richmond, VA

Shenandoah Valley Apple Pie

Preparation time: 60 minutes

5 or 6 grated apples
   (depending on size)
1 tablespoon lemon juice
3 eggs, beaten

½ stick butter, melted
½ teaspoon cinnamon
½ cup white sugar
1 unbaked 9-inch pie crust

Grate apples on a coarse grater; sprinkle lemon juice over apples. Beat eggs and add slightly cooled melted butter to eggs. Add cinnamon and sugar to egg and butter mixture. Add apples to mixture, stir lightly until well mixed. Pour into unbaked 9-inch pie crust, leave untopped. Bake at 350° for 40 minutes until browned and cooked through. Makes five to six servings.

Shirley Lipovac
Walnut Creek, CA

Shirley's Dessert

Preparation time: 40 minutes

3 eggs, beaten	½ cup chopped walnuts
1 cup sugar	¾ cup chopped dates
1 cup graham cracker crumbs	Tart jelly for topping

Mix first 5 ingredients; pour into 9-inch greased cake tin, bake at 350° for 25 to 30 minutes. Remove from oven, and while still warm, spread with tart jelly. Makes 1 9-inch cake pan.

Helen Robiolio
Union City, NJ

Stuffed Peaches for Two

Preparation time: approximately 1 hour

2 peaches (medium/ large), rinsed well	Sugar to taste
2 or 3 amaretti (Italian macaroons)	1 tablespoon of Marsala
	1 pat of butter

Split peaches in half, lengthwise, removing stones. Scoop out pulp, leaving an edge about ¼ inch around. Mix together the scooped-out pulp, amaretti, sugar and Marsala to make a smooth paste. Fill the peach cavities with this mixture, piling high in the middle. Dot with butter and bake at 375° for about 45 minutes. May be served hot or cold—alone or topped with whipped cream or ice cream. Makes 2 servings.

Ruth W. Godsey
Renton, WA

Yogurt Pudding

Preparation time: 1 hour

3 eggs, beaten
¼ cup yogurt (plain)
½ cup mild honey
½ teaspoon cinnamon
¼ teaspoon nutmeg
⅛ cup margarine
¾ cup wheat germ

Beat first five ingredients well and pour into a crust made of the margarine and wheat germ: cream the margarine and wheat germ together until completely mixed. You may add ¼ teaspoon salt (optional). Spread this mixture in the bottom of a glass pie pan (9-inch) evenly. Pour yogurt pudding mixture over it. Bake for 45 minutes at 325°. Serves two.

Busy people will go to great lengths *or* heights to bake a great torte. The top prize-winning Apple Torte, which also tied for Grand Prize in the contest, was baked by Pamela Bartlett of Stamford, Connecticut. Aside from baking pastries for her husband Robert, this Kelly Services branch office supervisor is also a student pilot and member of the "Three Wing Flying Club." You'll wow guests with this top torte, and with the other great breads, cookies, and treats in this chapter.

Ellen Greenwold
Huntingdon Valley, PA

All Night Kisses

Preparation time: 20 minutes, plus baking time

1 egg white
⅓ cup sugar
½ teaspoon vanilla
  Pinch salt
½ cup chocolate chips

½ cup coconut
⅛ teaspoon maple extract
½ cup chopped walnuts
  or pecans

Bake overnight, oven off.
Preheat oven to 350°. Beat egg white until foamy, add sugar and beat until stiff—add and mix together vanilla, salt, chips, coconut, maple extract and nuts. Line a large cookie sheet with aluminum foil and drop by teaspoon. Place cookie sheet on floor of oven. Turn heat off immediately. Leave in closed oven overnight or approximately 9 hours. Makes around 15 cookies. For more cookies, double recipe. If coconut or maple extract aren't available, they may be omitted.

Hermine S. Just
Wilton, CT

Angel Pie

Preparation time: 2 hours

4 egg whites
1 cup granulated sugar
1 teaspoon cream of tartar
  Pinch of salt
4 egg yolks
½ cup granulated sugar

Rind of one lemon
3 tablespoons lemon juice
½ pint heavy cream
1 tablespoon
  confectioners' sugar

(187)

Beat 4 egg whites until frothy. Add gradually, 1 cup granulated sugar, 1 teaspoon cream of tartar and pinch of salt. Beat until stiff. Pour into a well-buttered and -floured pie plate. Bake one hour at 275°. Cool. Meringue will be puffed up high but will fall as it cools. Beat 4 egg yolks. Add gradually ½ cup granulated sugar, grated rind of 1 lemon and 3 tablespoons lemon juice. Cook in double boiler until thick. Cool. Spread on top of meringue. Whip ½ pint heavy cream sweetened with 1 tablespoon confectioners' sugar. Cover pie with whipped cream. Chill until ready to serve.

Virginia Di Fronzo
Brooklyn, NY

Apple Puffs

Preparation time: 45 minutes

1½ cups all purpose flour
2½ teaspoons baking
    powder
½ cup sugar
¼ teaspoon salt
1 large tart apple, peeled
    and chopped
½ cup currants or seedless
    raisins

1 egg
¾ cup milk
¼ cup melted butter or
    margarine
2 tablespoons melted
    butter
    Cinnamon sugar

Sift dry ingredients. Mix in apple and currants. Beat egg lightly with milk and ¼ cup butter—stir milk mixture into flour mixture just until it combines. Fill greased 2- or 2½-inch muffin pans—⅔ full. Bake in 400° oven until golden brown—18 to 20 minutes for 2-inch muffins—for 2½-inch muffins—25 minutes. Remove while warm from pans. Brush tops with 2 tablespoons butter, then roll in cinnamon sugar to coat generously.

Cinnamon Sugar: Mix well ⅓ cup sugar and 1 teaspoon cinnamon. Makes 15 large muffins.

Pamela Bartlett
Stamford, CT

Apple Torte

Preparation time: 1 hour

½ cup margarine
⅓ cup sugar
¼ teaspoon vanilla
1 cup flour
1 package (8 ounces)
  cream cheese
¼ cup sugar

1 egg
½ teaspoon vanilla
⅓ cup sugar
½ teaspoon cinnamon
4 cups peeled apple slices
½ cup sliced almonds

Cream first three ingredients. Blend in flour. Spread dough onto bottom and sides of 9-inch spring pan. Combine softened cream cheese with ¼ cup sugar. Mix well. Add egg and vanilla and mix and pour into pastry-lined pan. Combine ⅓ cup sugar and cinnamon. Toss apples in sugar mixture. Spoon apple mixture over cream cheese layer; sprinkle with nuts. Bake at 450° for 10 minutes. Reduce heat to 400°. Continue baking for 25 minutes. Cool and remove rim from pan. Makes 8–10 servings.

Nancy Whitley
Torrance, CA

Best Bran Muffins

Preparation time: 35 minutes

¼ cup sugar
1 cup butter
1 teaspoon baking soda
1 cup buttermilk

½ cup flour
2 cups bran flakes
½ cup raisins
1 egg

Cream butter and sugar. Dissolve soda in the buttermilk and add to butter/sugar mixture. Stir in rest of ingredients. Spoon into hot greased muffin pans. Bake at 400° for 20 minutes. Let cool for at least 5 minutes before removing. Makes 2½ dozen.

Beth Schulman
Howard Beach, NY

Beth's Brownies

Preparation time: 1–1¼ hours

½ pound butter
2 cups sugar
4 ounces unsweetened chocolate, melted
4 eggs
1 teaspoon vanilla
½ cup flour

½ teaspoon salt
2 teaspoons baking powder
2 cups walnuts
1 cup bittersweet chocolate chips

Cream butter and sugar. Add chocolate to mixture and blend. Mix in eggs and vanilla. In separate bowl sift flour, salt, and baking powder. Add to mixture. Mix well. Add walnuts and chips. Mix well. Bake in long 11x13-inch pan for 50 minutes to 1 hour at 325°. Makes 20–30 brownies. Serve chilled for fudgy brownies.

Sally A. Hurlburt
Binghamton, NY

Blueberry Coffee Cake

Preparation time: 1 hour

- ¾ cup sugar
- ¼ cup margarine
- 1 egg
- ½ cup milk
- 1½ cups sifted flour
- 2 teaspoons baking powder
- ½ teaspoon salt
- 1 cup well-drained canned or fresh blueberries

Combine the above in order given. Spread with topping (below) before baking. Bake at 375° for 35–40 minutes.

Crumb topping:

- ½ cup sugar
- ½ cup flour
- ½ teaspoon cinnamon
- ¼ cup butter

Mix thoroughly.

Dee Vidick
Denver, CO

Butter Cookies

Preparation time: 15–20 minutes, plus chilling time

- 1 cup butter, softened
- 2 cups flour
- ½ cup sugar
- 1 cup finely chopped walnuts

Preheat oven to 350°. Mix thoroughly all ingredients. Refrigerate dough until well chilled. Roll dough ¼-inch thick. Cut into 1½-inch circles. Place on ungreased cookie sheet. Bake 10–12 minutes. If desired, sprinkle with confectioners' sugar or put cookies together in pairs with raspberry jam. Makes about 24 cookies.

Karen Blake
Torrance, CA

Carrot Bread

Preparation time: 1 hour, 15 minutes

2 eggs
1 cup sugar
⅔ cup oil
1½ cups flour
¾ teaspoon soda
1 teaspoon cinnamon
1 teaspoon nutmeg
½ teaspoon salt
1½ cups raw carrots, grated
1 cup walnuts
¾ cup raisins

Beat eggs and add sugar and oil. Sift together flour, soda, cinnamon, nutmeg and salt and add to egg mixture. Beat well. Add carrots, nuts and raisins. Grease 5 soup cans or one 9x5-inch loaf pan. Fill cans half full. Bake at 350° for 45 to 50 minutes for soup cans or 1 hour for loaf pan.

Marie Mykalcio
Ridgefield, CT

Cheese Bread

Preparation time: 2 hours

¾ cup warm milk
¼ cup vegetable or corn oil
1 tablespoon honey
3 eggs, beaten
2½ cups flour (whole wheat or white)
1 package active dry yeast
½ teaspoon salt (optional)
¼ cup toasted sesame seeds
2 cups grated Cheddar cheese (or any cheese to your taste that's similar)

Mix the milk, oil, honey and eggs. Mix half the flour, the yeast, salt, sesame seeds and cheese. Add flour mixture to milk mixture. Beat 3 or more minutes. Work in remaining flour by hand. Cover the dough, let rise for 1 hour. Place in a well oiled 9x5-inch loaf pan. Press extra sesame seeds into top of loaf. Bake 45 minutes at 350°. Cool. Makes 1 loaf.

Nancy G. Smith
Midland, TX

"Chews"

Preparation time: 1 hour

¾ cup flour
1 teaspoon baking powder
1 cup sugar
1 cup dates, chopped
1 cup pecans, chopped
2 eggs
Confectioners' sugar

In medium-size bowl, combine dry ingredients. Add chopped dates and pecans. Stir. Add eggs. You will have to mix this by hand. Pour mixture into greased and floured 9 x 9-inch pan. Bake at 350° for 30–35 minutes. Check doneness as you would with a cake. When done, remove from oven and cut into 1″ squares. With buttered hands, roll each square into unpacked balls while hot. Then roll each ball in powdered sugar. Makes about 28.

Karen Feinberg
Cincinnati, OH

Cinnamon Cookies

Preparation time: 65–70 minutes

1 cup butter or margarine	1 tablespoon milk
½ cup brown sugar, packed firm	2½ cups sifted all-purpose flour
½ cup white sugar	1 tablespoon cinnamon
1 egg	½ teaspoon salt

Coating:

½ cup white sugar
1½ teaspoons cinnamon
1–2 tablespoons flour

Preheat oven to 375°. Cream together butter, brown sugar, and white sugar. Add egg and milk and mix thoroughly. Sift together flour, cinnamon, and salt, and add gradually to first mixture. Mix thoroughly. In small bowl, mix sugar and cinnamon for coating. Form dough into walnut-sized balls and roll in bowl until coated with sugar-cinnamon mixture. Place on lightly buttered cookie sheets. Dip bottom of a glass into remaining flour and use it to flatten balls of dough to about ⅛-inch thickness. Bake at 375° for 10 minutes. Cool on rack. Makes about 4 dozen.

Coleen Cooper
New Canaan, CT

Cinnamon Flop

Preparation time: 35 minutes

1 cup sugar
2½ cups flour
2 tablespoons baking
powder
1 cup milk

1 egg
5 tablespoons melted
butter
1 cup brown sugar
Cinnamon

Sift sugar, flour, and baking powder. Add milk, egg, and 1 tablespoon butter. Mix thoroughly. Put in 2 greased 8-inch cake pans. Spread each with ½ cup brown sugar. Sprinkle with cinnamon and drop 2 tablespoons of melted butter on each pan, over sugar and cinnamon. Nuts may be added on top. Bake 20–25 minutes in a 350° oven. Makes 12–18 servings.

Claudia Patton
Glendale, CO

Cosmic Carrot Cake

Preparation time: 1 hour, 15 minutes

1 stick (½ cup) margarine
or butter
3 cups grated carrots
2 cups flour
2 cups sugar
1 teaspoon salt
2 teaspoons cinnamon

1 teaspoon pumpkin pie
spice, or ½ teaspoon
ginger and ½ teaspoon
nutmeg
1 teaspoon baking soda
2 eggs

Turn the oven on to 350°. Put the stick of margarine in a 13″ x 9″ pan and set it in the oven to melt. Grate the carrots into one bowl, and mix the dry ingredients in another bowl. Beat the eggs into the melted margarine, and then add the carrots and the dry ingredients, all into the cake pan; mix well. Bake at 350° for 30–40 minutes, or until a knife or toothpick inserted into the center comes out clean. Frost with Cream Cheese Frosting (below) when cool. Makes 12–16 servings.

Cream Cheese Frosting

2 packages (3 ounces each) of cream cheese
½ stick margarine or butter

2 cups powdered sugar, approximately
1 tablespoon vanilla

Leave the cream cheese and margarine at room temperature until soft, and then beat together. Gradually beat in the powdered sugar. Add the vanilla, and beat well.

Margaret Wagner
Redford Township, MI

Date and Nut Torte

Preparation time: 45 minutes

1 cup white sugar
5 tablespoons graham cracker crumbs (about 4 crackers)
1 teaspoon baking powder

9 dates, sliced thin
1 cup coarsely chopped nuts
3 beaten egg yolks
3 beaten egg whites

Combine first 6 ingredients. Fold in egg whites. Put in greased 8-inch square or 7 x 9-inch pan at 350° for 30 minutes or until fairly firm and brown. Serve cold with whipped cream or ice cream. Makes 10 servings.

Lucille Griffin
Des Moines, IA

Dilly Bread

Preparation time: 1½ hours

1 package yeast
¼ cup water
2 tablespoons sugar
1 cup warm cottage cheese
1 tablespoon butter

1 tablespoon dill seed
1 teaspoon salt
1 egg
¼ teaspoon baking powder
2½ cups flour

Mix yeast, water and sugar; set aside for 5 minutes. Stir remaining ingredients together in a large bowl. Add yeast mixture. Knead to form dough. Turn into buttered 1-quart casserole. Let rise 1 hour in warm place. Bake at 325° for 25 minutes, then 350° for 15–20 minutes, depending on your oven.

A unique tasting bread which stays moist. You really don't have to worry about it spoiling; it won't be around long to do that.

Dorothy Jackson
Racine, WI

Dorothy Jackson's Pound Cake

Preparation time: 1½ hours

3 cups powdered sugar
1 pound butter, softened
8 eggs
2 tablespoons vanilla flavor.

1 tablespoon mace
3 cups cake flour

Heat oven to 300°. Grease and flour baking pan, 9 x 5 x 3½-inches. Cream butter and sugar. Slowly add flour 1 cup at a time. Slowly add egg yolks to mixture. Beat at slow speed for 10 minutes. Then add egg whites, flavor and mace, beat another 5 minutes. Pour into pan. Bake until wooden pick inserted in center comes out clean. Approximately 1 hour. Let cool for 20–25 minutes.

Martha Winfield
Memphis, TN

Egg Twist Bread

Preparation time: 3 hours (includes time for dough to rise)

1 package active dry yeast	2 large eggs
1¼ cups warm water	4½ cups plain white flour
3 tablespoons sugar or honey	¼ cup cornmeal (optional)
	1 egg yolk
1 teaspoon salt	2 tablespoons poppy seeds
¼ cup cooking oil	

Dissolve yeast in water in large bowl. Add honey, salt, oil, eggs and mix. Add 2 cups flour, mix; continue adding flour until dough is easy to handle. Sprinkle rest of flour on pastry board and knead dough, mixing in rest of flour until it becomes smooth and elastic. (More or less flour may be needed depending upon size of eggs, weather, etc.) Using about ¼ cup more oil, grease 5-quart bowl, put dough in bowl, turn to coat both sides, cover with towel, let rise 45 minutes, in warm place. Oil a 14-inch cookie sheet. Sprinkle with cornmeal—set aside. When dough is double in size, punch down, separate into 3 pieces. Roll each piece in 18-inch length ropes and plait. Pinch together at each end. Place on cookie sheet to rise till double. Before baking at 350° till golden brown, spread the egg yolk on top of the loaf and sprinkle with poppy seeds. (Bake about 30 minutes till brown.) Makes one very large loaf that freezes well. Remove from freezer and cut off the portion needed and return to freezer until next need. Wrap the bread in foil and heat in oven. This dough makes excellent pizza dough. To make 4 small loaves, simply double recipe.

Marijo Caffey
Wayne, NJ

French Coffee Puffs

Preparation time: 30 minutes

⅓ cup butter
½ cup sugar
1 egg
½ cup sour cream
1½ cups flour
1½ teaspoons baking powder
½ teaspoon salt
½ teaspoon cinnamon
⅔ cup chopped dates
½ cup chopped nuts (optional)

Cream butter and sugar, add egg, then sour cream. Add dry ingredients, then dates and nuts. Fill greased "mini tins" ⅔ full. Bake at 375°, 20 minutes. While hot, dip in ½ cup melted butter, then roll in mixture of ½ cup sugar and 1 tablespoon cinnamon.

Valerie Ann Denghel
Birmingham, MI

Grandma's Sour Cream Cake

Preparation time: 70 minutes

- 1 stick margarine
- 1 cup dark brown sugar
- 1 egg
- 1 cup sour cream
- ½ teaspoon salt
- 1 teaspoon baking soda
- 1 teaspoon baking powder
- 1 teaspoon cocoa (heaping)
- 1 cup flour
- ¼ teaspoon vanilla
- 1 cup raisins
- ½ cup chopped walnuts
- Confectioners' sugar

Melt margarine, add brown sugar and mix till syrupy. Add egg and sour cream and mix. Combine salt, soda, baking powder, cocoa and flour. Add to margarine mixture, blending until smooth. Finally add the vanilla. Fold in the raisins (which have been soaked in boiling water to make them plump, and then drained) and chopped walnuts. Pour into a well-greased 8 x 8 x 2-inch pan and bake 50 minutes at 325°. When cool, dust with confectioners' sugar. Makes 12 servings.

Patricia J. Peyton
Houston, TX

Harvest Muffins

Preparation time: 30 minutes

- ¼ cup butter or margarine, softened
- ⅓ cup sugar
- 1 egg
- 1 cup sifted all-purpose flour
- ½ teaspoon baking soda
- ¼ teaspoon salt
- 1 cup pared apples, chopped fine
- ½ cup Cheddar cheese, grated
- ¼ cup chopped walnuts (if desired)

Cream butter with sugar. Add egg and beat well. Sift flour, baking soda and salt; add to butter mixture. Stir in apples, cheese, and nuts. Fill greased muffin tins ⅔ full. Bake at 350° for 20 minutes. Makes 6 muffins.

Gretchen Snyder
Elmhurst, NY

High Fiber Loaf

Preparation time: 1 hour, 15 minutes

2 cups whole wheat flour
1 cup white flour
  (preferably unbleached)
1 cup bran and/or whole
  grain cereal
½ cup unprocessed bran
1 teaspoon baking soda
2 teaspoons salt
1½ teaspoons baking
  powder
1 tablespoon cinnamon
¼ teaspoon ginger

1½ cups brown sugar
1¼ cups oil
4 eggs
2 teaspoons vanilla
1 tablespoon orange peel
2 cups grated carrots or
  zucchini
1 cup raisins, currants or
  dried papaya chips
2 tablespoons apple butter
1 cup chopped nuts

Measure dry ingredients into large bowl. Add oil, eggs, vanilla. Mix in remaining ingredients. Pour into two greased bread pans or four small (7¼ x 3½ x 2¼-inch) pans. Bake 1 hour at 350°.

Jessie Summers
Colton, CA

Honey-Carob Brownies

Preparation time: 45 minutes

1⅓ cups honey
1 cup salad oil
4 eggs
2 teaspoons vanilla extract
1 cup carob powder

1 cup nutmeats
1 cup raisins (optional)
2 cups whole wheat flour
(about)

Blend all ingredients in order given, adding only enough whole wheat flour to make a dough of a consistency to hold together. Turn dough into large, greased pan, 9 x 13-inches, and bake 25–30 minutes at 350°. Cut into two-inch squares. Do not overbake. Makes 25–30 brownies. The honey will pour out of the measuring cup easily if you measure the oil first, and use that cup without washing, for measuring honey.

Emma Hunter
Miami, FL

Hurry-up Coffee Cake

Preparation time: 40 minutes

1 egg
½ cup milk
2 tablespoons vegetable
oil
½ cup sugar

1 cup flour
2 teaspoons baking
powder
½ teaspoon salt

Topping:

½ cup brown sugar
1 teaspoon cinnamon
1 tablespoon flour

1 tablespoon melted
butter
½ cup finely chopped nuts

Preheat oven to 375°. Grease an 8-inch square pan. Beat egg and milk together. Add oil. Blend dry ingredients and stir into liquids. Mix with fork until thoroughly blended. Pour into prepared pan and sprinkle topping ingredients, which have been mixed together. Bake 20 to 25 minutes. Serve warm. Makes 8 servings.

Patricia Nolan
Oak Lawn, IL

Irish Bread

Preparation time: 1 hour, 15 minutes

1 cup raisins
1½ cups all-purpose flour
1½ teaspoons baking
powder
½ teaspoon salt
½ cup sugar
2 tablespoons lard
shortening

¾ cup milk
1 egg
3 teaspoons caraway
seeds
Nuts and fruits optional

Boil raisins for 3 minutes—drain and dust lightly with a little of the flour. Sift dry ingredients, flour, baking powder, salt, sugar. Rub in shortening with hands. Add milk, eggs, caraway seeds, raisins, nuts and fruits if desired. Pour into loaf pan, greased and floured. Bake in a preheated 350° oven for 1 hour.

Theresa B. Cordts
Landing, NJ

Italian Biscuits

Preparation time: 1 hour

2 pounds flour
3 heaping teaspoons
   baking powder

7 eggs
1 cup of sugar
1½ sticks melted butter

Put flour and baking powder in large bowl. Make a well in the middle of flour. Mix eggs in the middle of the well. Mix sugar and butter in eggs. Then a little at a time, mix flour into liquid. Keep mixing flour until thick. Then knead a little. Flour baking pan. Cut mixture into 4 long little loaves of bread and put in oven. Bake at 350° for 20 to 25 minutes or until slightly brown. Take out of oven and cut into pieces. Then put back in oven until pieces are slightly brown. Pieces are about ½-inch thick.

Jeanette Kater Nejame
North Miami Beach, FL

Johnny Bread

Preparation time: 45 minutes

1 egg (2 eggs for lighter
   bread)
⅛ teaspoon salt
1 cup milk
¼ cup lard, melted

¼ cup sugar
1 cup flour
2 teaspoons baking
   powder
1 cup corn meal

Beat egg well. Add salt, milk, lard and sugar and mix. Beat in the flour and baking powder and corn meal to form a very soft batter. Pour into greased 8 x 8-inch pan, well greased. Bake 30-35 minutes at 350°. Number of servings: According to cut size.

Judi Hutchins
Worcester, MA

Marmalade Bread

Preparation time: 1 hour, 20 minutes

2½ cups flour	½ cup orange marmalade
1 teaspoon baking soda	¼ cup vinegar
1 teaspoon salt	1 cup milk
¾ cup sugar	2 tablespoons melted
1 egg	shortening

Sift together first 4 ingredients. Combine egg and marmalade and stir in remaining ingredients. Pour liquid into a greased 9 x 5 x 3-inch pan, or 2 smaller ones. Bake 1 hour at 325°.

Virginia McCrae Patterson
Anchorage, AK

McCrae Clan Shortbread

Preparation time: 1 hour, 10 minutes

1 cup sugar
1 pound butter (Don't
cheat and use
margarine, it is worth
the extra cost!)
5 cups flour

Mix ingredients well (it is easiest with the butter at room temperature). Pat firmly into a 8½ x 11-inch pan. Bake at 350° for 1 hour. Cut into 1-inch squares while hot—it slices like butter. The true Scots may age their shortbread for 6 months or more, but some people can't wait until it is cool to eat it. This makes about 6 dozen.

Agnes Leach
Livonia, MI

Molasses Bran Muffins

Preparation time: 30 minutes

2¼ cups whole bran
1 cup milk plus 1
  tablespoon vinegar
⅓ cup molasses (dark)
¼ cup firmly packed
  brown sugar
1 egg

1 stick margarine, melted
  and cooled
1 cup regular flour
1 teaspoon baking powder
1 teaspoon soda
1 teaspoon salt
1 cup raisins

In a large bowl, combine bran, milk, molasses, and brown sugar. Let stand until liquid is absorbed. Stir egg and melted margarine into bran mixture. Combine remaining ingredients and add all at once; stir lightly, enough to moisten flour mixture evenly. Spoon into paper-lined medium-size muffin cups, filling each ⅔ full. Bake at 375°, 20 minutes. Let cool, or serve warm. Makes 12 muffins.

Jacqueline Goyette
Bloomfield Hills, MI

Mom's Old-Fashion Chocolate Chip Cookies

Preparation time: 25 minutes

2 sticks margarine
2 eggs
1 teaspoon vanilla
1 cup white sugar
1 cup firmly packed
  brown sugar
2 cups flour
1 teaspoon baking soda
¾ teaspoon baking powder

½ teaspoon salt
2 cups rolled oats
1 package (12 ounces)
  chocolate chips
Optional: Add coconut
and nuts if desired.
(For plain oatmeal
cookies leave out
chocolate chips.)

Cream together margarine, eggs, vanilla, and sugars. Add flour, soda, baking powder, and salt and mix in. Stir in remaining ingredients. Drop by teaspoonfuls onto greased baking sheets. Bake at 400° for 10 minutes. Makes 4-5 dozen.

Christine Valenza
Alameda, CA

Monday Rye Bread

Preparation time: 3 hours rising, 45 minutes baking, 15 minutes preparing

- 2 tablespoons dry yeast
- 1 cup warm water
- ⅔ cup hot water
- 2 tablespoons butter or margarine
- ½ cup molasses
- 1 teaspoon salt
- 1 tablespoon caraway seeds
- 1 tablespoon anise seeds
- 3 tablespoons fresh grated orange rind
- 2½ cups rye flour
- 3 cups unbleached white flour

Dissolve yeast in 1 cup warm water. In large bowl melt butter in hot water and add molasses, salt, seeds and orange rind, with yeast mixture being added last. Sift together flours. Add most of flour to liquid, stirring. Turn dough out on floured surface to knead. Knead till smooth and elastic, working in remaining flour. Place in greased bowl and let rise til double in size, about 1½ hours. Punch down and form into 2 round loaves on greased baking sheet. Let rise till double again. Bake 350° for 45 minutes. Makes 2 loaves (which freeze well).

Anne Howard
Burlington, MA

Onion Board

Preparation time: 40 minutes

2 medium-sized onions,
  sliced and separated
  into rings
3 tablespoons butter or
  margarine
1 loaf frozen bread
  dough, thawed

1 egg
8 ounces sour cream
½ teaspoon salt
1 teaspoon poppy seeds

Saute onions in butter until soft. Roll out bread dough to a 10 x 12-inch rectangle and place on a lightly oiled cookie sheet. Spoon onion on top of bread dough. Beat egg in small bowl, add sour cream and salt. Spoon over onion mixture. Sprinkle with poppy seeds and bake at 375° for 25 minutes or until topping is set. Slice and serve warm. Makes 8 servings.

Pam Behunin
Pasadena, CA

Peanut Butter Bake

Preparation time: 50 minutes

1 cup crunchy peanut
  butter
⅔ cup butter (soft)
1 tablespoon vanilla
2 cups brown sugar
3 eggs

1 cup flour
½ teaspoon salt
¾ cup powdered sugar
1 tablespoon butter
1 square chocolate

Mix peanut butter, butter and vanilla. Add sugar and eggs, add flour and salt. Spread in 8-inch square pan and bake at 350° for 35 minutes.

Icing:

Mix powdered sugar with tablespoon of water until smooth. Spread over cookies. Melt butter and chocolate squares. Drizzle over white icing, cool or refrigerate until firm. Makes 10–12 servings.

Laurie Short
Larkspur, CA

Peanut Butter Christmas Cookies

Preparation time: 25 minutes

2 cups sifted flour	1 pound candied fruit
½ teaspoon baking powder	½ cup peanut butter
⅓ teaspoon baking soda	¼ cup margarine
½ teaspoon cinnamon	½ cup honey
½ teaspoon nutmeg	2 beaten eggs

Mix dry ingredients together. Mix candied fruit, peanut butter, margarine, honey, and eggs. Combine all ingredients together. Drop by spoonfuls onto a greased baking sheet. Bake at 350° for 15 minutes or until golden brown. Makes about 18 large cookies.

Rosemarie Collins
River Forest, IL

Pecan Balls

Preparation time: 30–40 minutes

½ pound butter
4 tablespoons sugar
1 tablespoon vanilla
2 tablespoons water

2 cups flour
2 cups chopped pecans
(fine)
Powdered sugar

Cream butter and sugar. Add vanilla and water; blend in.
Add flour and nuts. Mix well. Roll into balls (about the
size of a walnut). Bake at 350° for 15–20 minutes. When
slightly cooled, roll in powdered sugar. Makes about 48
cookies.

Janice Myers
Arvada, CO

Piccadilly Bars

Preparation time: 1 hour

Brownie Mixture:

2 cups sugar
⅔ cup margarine
6 ounces cream cheese
3 squares unsweetened
chocolate, melted, or
¾ cup cocoa

4 eggs
1⅓ cups flour
1 teaspoon baking powder
½ teaspoon salt
2 teaspoons vanilla

Cheesecake Topping:

2 tablespoons margarine
8 ounces cream cheese
¼ cup sugar
1 tablespoon cornstarch

1 egg
2 tablespoons milk
½ teaspoon vanilla

Chocolate Icing:

2 tablespoons butter
3 tablespoons milk

6 ounces semi-sweet
chocolate chips

Brownie Mixture: Cream sugar, margarine, and softened cream cheese in a bowl. Add cocoa or melted chocolate. Stir in eggs with a wooden spoon, beating after each. Add dry ingredients and vanilla. Stir well. Spread in 9 x 13-inch greased cake pan. Cover with cheesecake topping before baking.

Cheesecake Topping: Cream margarine, cream cheese, sugar and cornstarch in a small, deep bowl. Add egg, milk, and vanilla. Beat at high speed on mixer until smooth and creamy. Gently spread over the brownie mixture. Bake at 350° for 30–40 minutes. A toothpick will come out clean.

Chocolate Icing: After bars are cooled they may be iced with the following chocolate icing: Heat in heavy saucepan over medium-low heat 2 tablespoons butter, 3 tablespoons milk, and 6 ounces semi-sweet chocolate chips. Stir until melted and either drizzle (lacelike) or spread over Piccadilly Bars. Cut and serve. Makes 24.

Leslie J. Levine
Cranston, NJ

Pineapple Banana Cake

Preparation time: 1½ hours

3 cups sifted flour
1 teaspoon baking soda
1 teaspoon cinnamon
2 cups sugar
1 teaspoon salt
1½ cups cooking oil

1 can (8 ounces) crushed
pineapple and juice
1½ teaspoons vanilla
3 eggs
2 cups diced ripe bananas

Mix and sift together dry ingredients. Add remaining ingredients and blend (not beat). Pour into greased 9-inch tube pan and bake at 350° for 1 hour and 20 minutes. Set aside to cool without removing from pan. No frosting is needed.

Judy McCabe
Colorado Springs, CO

Pineapple Cake with Sauce Topping

Preparation time: 1½ hours

2 eggs	1 teaspoon cinnamon
1½ cups sugar	1 can (#303) pineapple
2 cups flour	(may substitute can of
½ teaspoon salt	fruit cocktail)
2 teaspoons baking soda	½ cup brown sugar
½ teaspoon nutmeg	1 cup walnuts
½ teaspoon ground cloves	

Beat eggs and sugar until creamy. Sift together flour, salt, baking soda, nutmeg, cloves and cinnamon. Add to egg and sugar mixture. Add pineapple. Pour into a well-greased 13 x 9-inch baking pan. Sprinkle brown sugar and walnuts over batter. Bake for 1 hour at 300°. Let cool while making sauce.

Sauce:

½ cup sugar	1 cup evaporated milk
1 stick butter	1 teaspoon vanilla

Boil all ingredients for 5 minutes. Pour over warm cake.

Marilyn Michaelis
Arvada, CO

Pineapple Zucchini Bread

Preparation time: 1 hour, 15 minutes

3 eggs	3 cups flour
1 cup oil	2 teaspoons soda
2 cups sugar	1 teaspoon salt
1 teaspoon vanilla	½ teaspoon baking powder
2 cups zucchini, shredded	1½ teaspoons cinnamon
1 cup crushed pineapple, drained	¾ teaspoon nutmeg
	1 cup chopped nuts

Beat the eggs, oil and sugar until smooth and creamy. Stir in the vanilla, zucchini and pineapple. Sift together the dry ingredients and add to mixture. Add nuts, if desired. Bake for 1 hour at 350°. Makes 2 loaves

Pam Main
Bethany, OK

Quick Blueberry-Apple Delight

Preparation time: 40 minutes

1 egg	1½ cups sifted flour
½ cup milk	½ cup sugar
¼ cup vegetable oil or melted shortening	2 teaspoons baking powder
½ cup raw cubed tart apple (unpeeled)	½ teaspoon salt
½ cup fresh blueberries or ¾ cup canned (well drained)	½ teaspoon cinnamon

Prepare muffin tins—grease bottoms only! In mixing bowl, beat egg slightly with whisk or fork—add milk and oil—

beat till frothy—blend in fruit—sift all dry ingredients and add all at once to liquid measure—blending with fork until moistened *only*—Do not mix or stir—mixture should appear lumpy—fill muffin cups ⅔ full—bake until golden brown at 400° for 20–25 minutes—Best when served hot with butter and (or) pure golden honey. Makes 10–12 delights —Great for breakfast!

Linda A. Josifchuk
Denver, CO

Rocky Mountain Bran Muffins

Preparation time: 35 minutes

½ cup oil
1 cup brown sugar
1 egg
2 tablespoons molasses
½ cup flour
½ cup wheat germ
¼ cup sesame seeds
1 teaspoon baking soda

½ teaspoon salt
¼ teaspoon cinnamon
¼ teaspoon nutmeg
⅛ teaspoon ground cloves
1½ cups bran
½ cup raisins
1 cup buttermilk

Beat first four ingredients together well. Add remaining ingredients and beat together. Pour batter into paper muffin cups. Bake at 400° for 20–25 minutes. Makes about 16 muffins.

Cathy Payne
Philadelphia, PA

Russian Coffee Cake

Preparation time: 1 hour, 15 minutes

½ pound butter (creamed)
1 cup sugar
1 teaspoon vanilla
3 eggs
2 cups flour
3 teaspoons baking
powder

1 teaspoon baking soda
½ pint sour cream
1 cup brown sugar
½ cup chopped nuts
2 teaspoons cinnamon

In a bowl mix first four ingredients by hand or mixer then add next four ingredients. Combine brown sugar, nuts, and cinnamon for topping. Pour ½ of batter in a greased, floured tube pan then put half of topping, then add rest of batter on top and sprinkle with rest of the topping. Bake at 350° for 45 minutes to an hour; test with a toothpick; it is done when toothpick comes out clean.

Agnes Bass
St. Louis, MO

Strawberry Bread

Preparation time: 1½ hours

3 cups all-purpose flour
2 cups sugar
1 teaspoon baking soda
1 teaspoon salt
1½ teaspoons cinnamon
2 packages (10 ounces
each) frozen
strawberries (thawed)

1¼ cups cooking oil
1¼ cups pecans
4 well-beaten eggs

Sift first 5 ingredients together into large bowl, make a well in center. Mix remaining ingredients well and add to the bowl. Mix slowly and thoroughly with flour mixture. Pour into 2 well-greased loaf pans and bake 1 hour at 350° until bread springs back when touched in center. Makes 2 loaves.

Jo Ann Patterson
Edinburg, IL

Sugar Crusted Raisin Bars

Preparation time: 40 minutes

1 egg	½ teaspoon baking powder
⅔ cup brown sugar	¼ teaspoon salt
⅓ cup salad oil	1 teaspoon vanilla
1 cup sifted flour	¾ cup raisins

Topping:

2 tablespoons granulated
   sugar
½ teaspoon cinnamon

Preheat oven to 350°. Beat egg lightly and stir in sugar and oil. Sift together flour, baking powder and salt. Add to first mixture and blend well. Stir in vanilla and raisins. Spread in a greased 9-inch square pan. Stir topping ingredients together and sprinkle over the batter. Bake about 25 minutes. Cool. Cut into 24 bars.

Susan Reinhart
Fullerton, CA

Versatile Health Bread

Preparation time: 1 hour

¼ cup softened butter
¼ cup honey
2 eggs, lightly beaten
¾ cup plain yogurt
1 cup whole wheat flour
1 cup all-purpose flour

2 teaspoons baking
 powder
½ teaspoon baking soda
½ teaspoon salt
¼ cup wheat germ

Cream together first four ingredients. Add dry ingredients to creamed mixture. Pour into greased bread pan and bake at 350° for 35–45 minutes or until golden brown.

Substitute for yogurt:

1 cup mashed bananas and 1⅝ ounces poppy seeds
 or
1 cup grated carrots, ½ cup chopped dates, allspice,
  cloves
 or
1 cup applesauce, ½ cup bran buds, cinnamon, nutmeg
 or
1 cup raisins, 1 tablespoon caraway seeds
 or
½ cup cranberry sauce, ½ cup walnuts
1 tablespoon orange rind, cinnamon, cloves
 or
1 cup shredded zucchini, ½ cup carrots

Philip C. Stoehr
Rutherford, NJ

Walnut Cocoons

Preparation time: 25 minutes

1 cup butter or margarine	1 cup chopped walnuts
4 tablespoons confectioners' sugar	(or pecans)
1 teaspoon water	Extra confectioners' sugar
⅛ (scant) teaspoon salt	Chocolate pieces
1 teaspoon vanilla extract	(optional)
2 cups flour	

Soften butter in large bowl. Beat butter, 4 tablespoons confectioners' sugar, water, salt and vanilla extract until fluffy. Beat in flour and nuts; mix well. Form 2-inch cocoon shapes by rolling between palms; place on ungreased cookie sheet. Bake at 375° about 13 minutes, until lightly browned on bottom. Remove to wire rack, cool 1 minute. Roll immediately in confectioners' sugar and again just before serving. Yields 40 cookies. Variation: divide dough into 40 equal parts. Shape each piece around chocolate "kiss" to cover completely, forming a ball. Continue as above.

Anita Chandler
Sumner, WA

Whole Wheat English Muffins

Preparation time: 3 hours

2 tablespoons sugar	1½ cups whole wheat flour
1 teaspoon salt	¼ cup cracked wheat
3 tablespoons butter	⅓ cup wheat germ
1 cup milk, scalded	3 cups (approx.) white flour
1 cup warm potato water	
1 package dry yeast	

Add sugar, salt and butter to scalded milk. Cool to luke-warm. Put potato water in large mixing bowl. Add yeast and dissolve. Add cooled milk mixture, whole wheat flour, cracked wheat, wheat germ and 1 cup white flour. Beat until smooth. Add enough white flour to make a stiff dough. Knead on lightly floured board for 2 minutes or until the dough is manageable. Put in greased bowl turning-to grease top, cover and let rise until double. Punch down and divide in half. Roll, half at a time, ½-inch thick and cut in 3-inch rounds. Put on cookie sheets lightly sprinkled with corn meal. Cover and let rise until doubled. Heat a lightly oiled skillet or griddle, preferably cast iron, over low heat. Put 3 or 4 muffins on skillet and cook *slowly*, browning well on both sides. Ten minutes per side is about right. Remove to wire rack and cool. Makes 18–20.

Alexandra McCorkle
Collegeville, PA

Wholesome Banana Nut Bread

Preparation time: 1½ hours

¾ *cup margarine (corn oil)*
1 *cup sugar (¾ cup firmly packed brown and ¼ cup white sugar)*
3 *eggs*
3 *cups flour (2 cups whole wheat and 1 cup white-unbleached)*
½ *cup wheat germ or bran (unprocessed)*

1 *tablespoon baking powder*
1 *teaspoon baking soda*
1 *teaspoon salt*
¾ *cup milk*
2 *tablespoons lemon juice*
2 *cups mashed bananas (ripe)*
1 *cup chopped nuts (walnuts or pecans)*

Prepare: 2 baking pans—8½ x 4½ x 2½-inches—greased and lightly floured. Set oven at 350°. In a large bowl, cream together margarine and sugar. Add eggs one at a time and

(219)

beat thoroughly after each egg. Add alternately, combined dry ingredients and milk thoroughly after each addition. Combine mashed bananas with lemon juice and fold in thoroughly. Add chopped nuts and mix evenly through batter. Pour mixture into baking pans and put in oven for 50 to 60 minutes or until cake tester or narrow toothpick comes out clean from center. Let cool in pans for 15 minutes. Holding pan, gently shake to loosen bread from sides or slide cook knife around the edges to loosen. Turn out bread and cool on wire rack. Can be served fresh or wrap and store in freezer. Makes 2 loaves.

de'Lane LaPicca
Jonesboro, AR

Working Girl's Fabulous Hot Rolls

Preparation time: 2½–3 hours, plus refrigeration time

- 6 tablespoons sugar
- 1 stick margarine
- 1 teaspoon salt
- ½ cup water
- 1 envelope powdered yeast
- ½ cup lukewarm water
- 1 egg
- 3 cups unsifted flour

Combine sugar, margarine, salt and ½ cup water in saucepan over low heat to melt margarine. Cool to lukewarm. Dissolve yeast in ½ cup lukewarm water; add to first mixture. Beat the egg and add to above. Stir in the unsifted flour. Cover with wax paper and refrigerate several hours or overnight. Roll out on lightly floured board, cut and place about 1-inch apart on greased cookie sheets. Let rise about 2 hours in warm place. Bake at 375° until light golden brown, about 15 minutes.

Note: Be sure water and margarine mixture are luke-warm. Too hot will kill the yeast, too cool will not activate it. This recipe is great for making ahead because it will keep several days in refrigerator, and you can take out a small amount of dough at a time for however many rolls you need and store the rest. The best thing about my recipe is that there is no kneading and you don't go through all the punching down steps. I usually take some dough and cut my rolls out when I get home from work and let them set until time for dinner. Makes 12 rolls. To increase recipe for a crowd, just double ingredients.

Louise Smothers
Olathe, KS

Yum-Yum Snack Bars

Preparation time: 40 minutes

2 cups old-fashioned
  rolled oats, uncooked
¼ cup sesame seed
½ cup chopped nuts
¼ cup wheat germ
2 tablespoons vegetable
  oil

⅔ cup honey
1 egg
⅓ cup smooth peanut
  butter

Combine oats, sesame seed, nuts, and wheat germ in large mixing bowl. Beat together oil, honey, egg, and peanut butter. Add to oats mixture and blend well. Spread in 8 x 8-inch baking dish which has been greased. Bake at 300°, 20–25 minutes or until lightly browned. Cut into bars. Let cool in dish. Makes about 16 bars. Delicious with milk.

Mary Ellen King
Cocoa Beach, FL

Zucchini Bikini Bread
(Serve barely covered with butter or cream cheese)

Preparation time: 90 minutes

1 cup sifted all-purpose flour	½ cup raisins
1 cup whole wheat flour	1 cup chopped dried apricots
½ teaspoon baking powder	3 eggs
2 teaspoons baking soda	½ cup vegetable oil
½ teaspoon salt	½ cup orange juice
3 teaspoons cinnamon	1 cup honey
½ cup wheat germ	2 cups peeled and grated zucchini
2 cups chopped walnuts or pecans	

Combine flours, baking powder, soda, salt, cinnamon, wheat germ, nuts, raisins, and apricots and blend thoroughly. In large bowl, beat eggs until foamy. Add oil, orange juice, and honey, and blend well. Stir in zucchini. Gradually stir in flour mixture. Pour into two greased loaf pans or a greased and floured Bundt cake pan. Bake in 325° oven for 1 hour or until center is firm when pressed with fingertip. Cool in pan for 5–10 minutes, remove and cool completely. May be served immediately—plain, or with butter or cream cheese, or may be wrapped and stored in refrigerator or freezer. Makes 2 loaves.

Brown Bag

This unusual recipe group is ideal for efficient Kelly Services people, interested in saving time, money, and doing the lunch-making job well. The winning special in this category, Eggy Yogurt Sandwich, reflects the current interest in nutrition, from filling to whole wheat bread. The Brown-Bagger is Pamela Schultz of Birmingham, Michigan—whose mother, a Kelly Girl employee too, also entered the "Recipes for Busy People" contest.

Joanne Takayo Angell
Wichita, KS

Born Again Reuben

Preparation time: 15 minutes

Dijon mustard
4 slices dark rye bread
¼ pound pastrami, sliced
  thin
¼ pound Swiss cheese,
  sliced thin

½ cup cabbage, sliced
  thin
4 tablespoons commercial
  coleslaw dressing
Pepper, coarse grind,
  to taste

Spread mustard on 2 slices of bread. Divide pastrami and cheese into two equal portions. Layer one portion pastrami, then cheese on 1 slice bread with mustard. Place half of cabbage on top of cheese. Pepper to taste. Top with 2 tablespoons dressing. Place plain slice of bread over to make sandwich. Repeat with other sandwich. Can be eaten as is but is excellent when placed in 350° oven until cheese melts or in microwave oven on high for one minute. Serves 2.

Cyndi Albrecht
Des Moines, IA

Carrot Salad

Preparation time: 20 minutes

½ cup grated carrots
½ cup chopped celery
½ cup chopped apple
¼ cup raisins

¼ cup chopped walnuts
Mayonnaise to moisten
  (3 teaspoons)
Salt to taste

Mix all ingredients together, salting to taste. Pack in small lidded containers for "brown bagging." (Chilling improves the flavor.) Serves 2 (generously). Yield: 2 cups.

Bonnie Lambert
Macon, GA

Egg Salad Spread

Preparation time: 10 minutes plus chilling time

3 *hard-cooked eggs, finely chopped*
½ *cup cottage cheese*
1 *tablespoon dairy sour cream*
2 *teaspoons prepared mustard*
1½ *teaspoons chopped onion*
¼ *teaspoon salt, or to taste*
⅛ *teaspoon Worcestershire sauce*
⅛ *teaspoon dill weed*

In small bowl combine eggs, cottage cheese, sour cream, mustard, onions, salt, Worcestershire sauce and dill weed. Cover and chill to blend flavors. Serve on rye or whole wheat bread. Yields: 1¼ cups.

Pamela J. Schultz
Birmingham, MI

Eggy Yogurt Sandwich

Preparation time: 5 minutes

1 *hard-boiled egg, chopped*
2 *tablespoons plain yogurt*
1 *teaspoon minced onion*
2 *black olives, chopped*
1 *teaspoon lemon juice*
½ *teaspoon parsley, chopped*
Salt and pepper
2 *slices whole wheat bread*
Lettuce leaves

Mix first 6 ingredients together; add salt and pepper to taste. Spread on whole wheat bread, top with lettuce. Yield: ⅓ cup filling, or one sandwich.

Pam Main
Bethany, OK

Fre-Man Lunch

Preparation time: 35 minutes

1 *loaf slightly stale French or Italian bread*	½ *cup diced Colby Cheddar cheese*
1 *cup chopped leftover turkey breast or deli turkey loaf*	½ *cup mayonnaise (or just enough to moisten ingredients)*
1 *small diced tomato*	*Shredded lettuce*
1 *medium diced green pepper*	¼ *teaspoon butter salt*
2 *stalks diced celery*	¼ *teaspoon paprika*

Prepare bread. Cut loaf in half, lengthwise and crosswise, and scrape about ¼ out of top half only. Prepare turkey and other ingredients, dice finely. Combine remaining ingredients except lettuce. Mix well. Stuff the hollowed pieces of bread with mixture. A light spread of mayonnaise on the bottom half of bread may be needed if it is too dry. Finish sandwich with lettuce. Wrap in foil (not too tight) and seal. To finish lunch, add sweet pickles and a nice juicy apple. Sandwiches may be stored overnight in refrigerator for ease of preparation. If sandwiches are to be heated, leave lettuce off until after heating. Makes 2 Fre-man Lunches.

Bernadine Pogreba
Omaha, NE

Fruit and Zucchini Bars

Preparation time: 1 hour

¾ cup soft margarine
2 eggs
1 teaspoon vanilla
½ cup brown sugar
½ cup white sugar
1¾ cups sifted flour
½ teaspoon salt

1½ teaspoons baking powder
¾ cup each raisins, coconut and snipped dates
2 cups grated zucchini

Icing:

1 teaspoon vanilla
¼ teaspoon cinnamon

1 cup powdered sugar
Cream to moisten

Beat together until creamy, margarine, eggs, vanilla and sugars. Blend together flour, salt and baking powder. Mix all together along with raisins, coconut, dates and zucchini. Bake in greased 9 x 13-inch pan for 35–40 minutes at 350°. Place on rack to cool slightly. Beat together icing ingredients. Drizzle over warm bars. Sprinkle with 1 cup finely chopped nuts. Cut into squares. Makes 24 bars.

Sheri Macfarlane
North Burnaby, Canada

Haystacks

Preparation time: 40–45 minutes

- 2 tablespoons water
- 3 cups dates
- 1½ cups of raisins (optional)
- ½ cup orange, apple or pineapple juice
- 4 cups unsweetened shredded, fine coconut
- ¾ cup whole wheat flour
- ⅓ cup old-fashioned rolled oats
- 1⅔ cups walnuts (pieces or chopped)
- ¼ teaspoon salt

Blend water, dates, raisins, juice in blender or food processor until smooth. Add to remaining ingredients in a bowl. Mix well. Scoop onto ungreased cookie sheet with ice cream scoop, or shape into uniform balls with hands. Bake until browned, 20–25 minutes at 350°. Makes 2½ to 3 dozen.

Variations: You can use various types of fruit rather than the 3 cups of dates. For example, use 1 cup dates, 1 cup prunes, 1 cup apples. Add some peanut butter for variation. Walnuts too expensive? Throw in some granola instead. Substitute bran or wheat germ for whole wheat flour.

Barbara J. Setnicker
Waterville, OH

Mini Meat Pies

Preparation time: 40 minutes

½ pound lean ground beef
½ onion, diced
½ green pepper, diced
1 egg
2 tablespoons catsup

Garlic salt to taste
Pepper
3 tablespoons rolled oats
1 can refrigerated
buttermilk biscuits

Mix all ingredients except biscuits (or make your favorite meatloaf recipe minus breadcrumbs or filler). Shape meat mixture into size of small golf balls and place on waxed paper while you open can of biscuits. Flatten out each biscuit (dough) and reshape into a square. Put a meatloaf ball in the center of each square, bring up corners and press to seal, completely covering each meatloaf ball with biscuit dough. Place on a greased cookie sheet, piercing each "pie" twice with a fork to create steam vents for cooking. Place in a 375° oven until brown (approximately 15–20 minutes). Makes 2 servings.

Tip: These mini meat pies can be chilled when there are leftovers, and packed for lunch with a piece of fruit and some cookies—hot or cold they're great!

Maryann Zepp
Lansdale, PA

Miniature Fruit Cheesecake

Preparation time: 1 hour

3 packages (8 ounces
each) cream cheese
1½ cups sugar
5 eggs

2 teaspoons vanilla
1 cup sour cream
Jelly

Cream the cheese, 1 cup sugar, 5 eggs and 1½ teaspoons
vanilla. Pour into paper cupcake cups in muffin tins and
bake at 300° for 30 to 35 minutes. Remove from oven and
cool 5 minutes. Mix the sour cream, ½ teaspoon vanilla
and ½ cup sugar. Spoon a spoonful of this topping atop
each cupcake. Place ¼ teaspoon of jelly on top. Return to
the oven and bake an additional 5 minutes. Cool and then
refrigerate or freeze. Makes 24 cupcakes.

Darlene Kenworthy
Chantilly, VA

The Economical Energizing Sandwich

Preparation time: 20 minutes

2 hard-boiled eggs,
mashed
1 can (6½ ounces) flaked
tuna (cheapest you can
buy), drained
¼ cup grated carrots
2 tablespoons chopped
onion
¼ cup chopped celery
1 teaspoon finely chopped
green pepper

¼ cup chopped peanuts or
cashews
⅓ cup mayonnaise
1 teaspoon curry powder
Salt and pepper to taste
6 buttered rolls, or 12
slices bread
Lettuce or spinach leaf
per sandwich

Mash the eggs in a medium mixing bowl. Add tuna, carrots, onion, celery, green pepper and nuts. Stir until evenly distributed. Blend curry powder into mayonnaise. Add to the tuna mixture. Spread onto buttered bread or buns and chill in refrigerator overnight. Add lettuce or spinach right before eating. Yields 6 sandwiches; 1⅔ cups filling.

Norma Kent Kerr
Anchorage, AK

Tuna Combo

Preparation time: 10 minutes plus marinating time

1 can (6½ ounces) tuna fish, drained	½ teaspoon garlic salt
1 tomato, chopped	½ teaspoon basil
2–3 olives, chopped	½ teaspoon olive oil
	1 fresh lemon

Combine the first six ingredients. Squeeze a fresh lemon over the mixture. Let marinate during the morning. Ready to eat at lunch time. Makes about 2 cups, or 1 generous serving.

Herb Chicken with Julienne Vegetables, first prize in this group, is typical of the delectable recipes in this chapter. Slender Katherine Cunningham, a full-time student at Boston College who works on Kelly temporary assignments during her summer vacations, cooked up this delight. Because she is "always on a diet," Ms. Cunningham says that she's especially interested in finding new ways to prepare appealing low-calorie dishes. Her ambition? To own and operate a restaurant catering service!

Mary Severine
San Diego, CA

Chicken Tomato-Broccoli

Preparation time: 20 minutes

2 large chicken breasts,
boned and cut in strips
3 tablespoons soy sauce
1 tablespoon vegetable oil
1 package (10 ounces)
frozen broccoli cuts,
thawed
1 cup chicken broth
1 can (6 ounces) water
chestnuts, drained and
sliced

5 fresh mushrooms, cut
into "T" shapes
1 tablespoon lemon juice
1 tablespoon cornstarch
Dash of garlic powder
1 large tomato, finely
diced

Combine chicken, soy sauce and vegetable oil in a small bowl. Set aside. Place broccoli and ½ cup of broth in a large skillet or wok. Cook over medium-high heat for 5 minutes, stirring frequently. Push to outer edge of skillet. Increase heat, and add chicken mixture. Cook until chicken loses its pink color, stirring frequently. Push to outer edge of skillet. Add water chestnuts and cook for 1 minute. Add mushrooms and cook 1 minute. Toss skillet mixture and remove from heat. Combine lemon juice and cornstarch. Stir into remaining ½ cup of broth. Stir into skillet mixture and heat until bubbly. Season with garlic powder. Just before serving, stir in diced tomatoes. Makes 2 generous servings. May be served over cooked rice for non-dieters.

Beth Putnom
Ontario, CA

Creamy Salad Dressing

Preparation time: 5 minutes

- ⅓ cup buttermilk
- 2 tablespoons small curd cottage cheese
- ¼ teaspoon salt
- ¼ teaspoon coarse black pepper
- ¼ teaspoon French's mustard
- 2 scallions, including green part, sliced
- 1 tablespoon minced parsley

Put all the ingredients in an electric blender and whirl until smooth. Makes ⅔ cup dressing.

Olga Wightwick
New Orleans, LA

Curried Crab Grapefruit

Preparation time: 10 minutes

- 1 grapefruit or 1 cup canned grapefruit sections
- 2 cans (6½ ounces each) crab meat
- 1 cup diced celery
- 2 teaspoons capers
- ¼ cup diet mayonnaise
- ½ teaspoon curry powder
- ¼ teaspoon salt

Mix and serve. If the ingredients have been kept in the refrigerator then it's not necessary to lose time in chilling. Makes 4 cups, or about 6 servings.

Carol C. Ellis
Orlando, FL

Flounder Fillets a la Moutarde

Preparation time: 10 minutes

2 tablespoons imitation mayonnaise	2 teaspoons chopped fresh parsley
1 tablespoon Dijon-style mustard	1 pound flounder fillets
	2 lemon wedges

In a small cup, combine mayonnaise, mustard and parsley; set aside. Broil flounder fillets on a rack, about 6 inches from source of heat, about 5 minutes or until fish is opaque and beginning to flake when tested with a fork. Pierce fillets lightly and spread evenly with mayonnaise mixture. Return to broiler for 1 minute. Garnish with lemon wedges. Makes 2 servings.

Jane Seelinger
Albuquerque, NM

Gazpacho

Preparation time: 10–15 minutes, plus chilling time

2 ribs celery	¼ teaspoon black pepper
1 bell pepper, seeded	3 tablespoons wine vinegar
1 cucumber, peeled and seeded	2 tablespoons parsley
1 medium onion, peeled	1 teaspoon chives
2 fresh tomatoes, peeled and diced	2 tablespoons olive oil
1 teaspoon salt	1 can (14 ounces) tomato juice

Coarsely chop first 5 ingredients and mix. Add next 7 ingredients and mix thoroughly. Chill 4 hours. Makes 8 servings, with about 72 calories per serving.

Katherine Cunningham
Newton, MA

Herb Chicken with Julienne Vegetables

Preparation time: 1 hour

- 2 chicken breasts, skin removed
- 2 medium zucchini, cut in julienne strips
- 4 medium carrots, cut in julienne strips
- 1 medium onion, sliced
- 1 cup chicken broth (made with 1 cup boiling water and 2 chicken bouillon cubes)

- 2 tablespoons dried parsley flakes
- 2 teaspoons sweet basil
- 1 bay leaf, whole
- ½ teaspoon seasoned pepper

Place skinned chicken in small casserole or baking dish and surround with vegetables. Pour chicken broth over all, and sprinkle with seasonings. Bake covered in 375° oven for 45 minutes or until tender. Serves 2.

Billie R. Locke
Nashville, TN

Low-Cal Cheesecake Citric Ice Cream

Preparation time: 20 minutes, plus freezing time

1 egg white
2 teaspoons concentrated lemon juice
4 tablespoons sugar
1 cup low-fat ricotta cheese
¾ cup half and half
1 cup plain yogurt

¼ teaspoon grated lemon rind
¼ teaspoon grated orange rind
¼ teaspoon grated lime rind
½ teaspoon vanilla extract

Beat egg white with lemon juice until it peaks. Beat in sugar gradually until stiff. In separate bowl, beat ricotta cheese with half and half and yogurt until it is smooth, fold in grated rinds, vanilla and then the beaten egg whites. Pour into a 1-quart serving bowl and freeze overnight. When serving, garnish rim of sherbert dish with a twist of any of the above fruits. About 100 calories per ½ cup. Makes 8 servings.

Kathleen Barger
Hillsboro, OR

Mock Potato Salad

Preparation time: 15 minutes

2 green onions
½ cup plain yogurt
¼ cup finely chopped celery
2 cups cooked cauliflower (just until tender)

1 hard-cooked egg, thinly sliced
Sprigs of parsley

Chop onions in small pieces; combine with yogurt and celery. Gently mix with cauliflower and eggs. Garnish with parsley. Pass freshly ground pepper. Serves 2.

Janet L. Vidick
Denver, CO

Stuffed Cherry Tomatoes

Preparation time: 15 minutes

24 cherry tomatoes	1 teaspoon chives
1 can (3¾ ounces) tuna (water packed)	½ teaspoon prepared mustard
2 tablespoons plain yogurt	¼ teaspoon salt

Slice off tops of cherry tomatoes; scoop out insides. Sprinkle insides with salt and pepper. Chill. Drain tuna and mix with yogurt, chives, mustard and salt. Fill tomatoes with mixture and chill. Makes 6 appetizer servings.

Rosemary Virden
Richmond, VA

Vanilla Lemon Frost

Preparation time: Approximately 3 hours

⅔ cup instant nonfat dry
milk

2 cups water

1 envelope unflavored
gelatin

½ cup sugar

2 egg whites

1 tablespoon grated
lemon rind

3 tablespoons lemon juice

1 tablespoon vanilla
extract

Dissolve dry milk in water. In a medium saucepan, mix gelatin with sugar; stir in milk. Cook over low heat, stirring constantly until gelatin and sugar are dissolved. Turn into a freezer tray without ice-cube divider. Freeze until frozen 1 inch from edge. Turn into a large bowl and add egg whites, lemon rind, lemon juice and vanilla. Beat at high speed for two minutes or until light and fluffy. Return to freezer tray; freeze until firm. Allow to soften slightly at room temperature before serving. Only 82 calories per ½ cup portion. Makes 1 quart.

Marinated Flank Steak is a hearty winner for busy cooks —it grills in less than 10 minutes! This version marinates in a tasty mix with a spirited secret, shared now by Kathleen Spolarich of Arlington, Virginia. She has worked in a variety of jobs with more than 20 companies since she joined Kelly Services in 1977. The wife of a Navy Lieutenant Commander, Kathleen has traveled throughout the country, trying recipes all the way. "I am very interested in new dishes, especially those which are simple and have the working family in mind," she says.

Johnell Lambe
Fresno, CA

Barbecued Chuck Roast

Preparation time: About 1 hour, plus marinating time

4½–5 pounds chuck roast
2 teaspoons meat
  tenderizer
½ cup oil
½ cup tomato ketchup
¼ cup red wine
2 tablespoons wine
  vinegar

2 cloves garlic, minced
½ teaspoon salt
½ teaspoon pepper
½ teaspoon dry mustard
½ teaspoon celery salt
½ teaspoon chili powder

Sprinkle roast with meat tenderizer; pierce with a fork at about ½-inch intervals. Combine remaining ingredients and pour over meat in a large bowl. Marinate roast for at least 4 hours, turning several times. Place roast on grill close to a hot barbecue fire and brown on both sides. Raise the grill a little and cook roast 20–25 minutes on each side depending on heat of the fire and of rareness you wish. Baste frequently. Makes 12–16 servings.

Chuck Blackburn
Carson, CA

Barbecued Crab-Stuffed Chicken Breast

Preparation time: 1 hour

4 whole boned chicken
  breasts
  Salt, pepper
1 cup crab meat
¼ cup chopped celery
¼ cup chopped green
  onions

Lemon pepper to taste
½ can frozen orange juice
¼ cup sherry wine
¼ cup honey

Salt and pepper boned chicken. Mix crab meat, celery, onions, and lemon pepper; stuff chicken breasts. Secure with skewers. Combine remaining ingredients to make a marinade. Place chicken on grill and broil over hot coals, basting frequently with marinade. Makes 4 servings.

Marian E. Hite
Swedesboro, NJ

Beat the Heat Delight

Preparation time: 2–3 hours

1 can (6 ounces) frozen orange juice concentrate	2 pounds boneless veal (or lamb) cut in 1-inch cubes
½ cup honey	
¼ cup chopped crystallized ginger	1 medium squash, cut into 2-inch pieces
¾ teaspoon marjoram leaves	4 medium apples, quartered

Mix orange juice concentrate, honey, ginger and marjoram. Place meat in shallow glass dish; pour orange juice mixture over meat. Cover; refrigerate several hours, turning meat occasionally. Cook squash in 1 inch boiling salted water, about 10 minutes. Drain. Remove meat from marinade; reserve marinade. On 6 skewers, alternate squash, apples, and meat. Place on grill. Cook 30 minutes or until meat is brown, and apples and squash are tender, turning and basting with remaining marinade. Serve over brown rice. Makes 4 servings.

Joanne Takayo Angell
Wichita, KS

Cinnamon Spareribs

Preparation time: 1½ hours, plus marinating time

2 pounds spareribs
½ teaspoon salt
2 tablespoons sugar

1 teaspoon cinnamon
2 tablespoons soy sauce
1 clove garlic (crushed)

Cut meat into two-rib servings. Place in 13 x 9 x 2-inch baking dish. Combine remaining ingredients and pour over ribs, covering well. Marinate at least 1 hour. Bake in same dish for 1¼ hours at 350°, basting occasionally if desired. Makes 2 servings. (Optional: parboil ribs for 15 minutes before marinating.)

Jessica Stewart
Tigard, OR

Dad's Pineneedle Sauce

Preparation time: 10 minutes

⅔ cup vegetable oil
⅔ cup lemon juice or
  vinegar
¼ cup water
1 tablespoon sugar
2 teaspoons salt
1 teaspoon MSG

1 teaspoon paprika
1½ teaspoons dried leaf
  tarragon
½ teaspoon dried leaf
  rosemary
¼ teaspoon Tabasco sauce
1 tablespoon minced onion

Combine all ingredients. Mix well. If desired, let stand at least an hour for flavors to blend. Use as a baste for barbecued chicken, spooning over as chicken cooks. Makes 1⅔ cups, enough for 4 broiler-fryer chickens. Can be stored in a covered jar, unrefrigerated, for a few weeks.

Raenell Agnew
North Palm Beach, FL

Dr. John's Bar-B-Q Sauce

Preparation time: 1 hour

2 sticks butter
8 cloves garlic, minced
6 tablespoons cider
vinegar
1 bottle (28 ounces) catsup
2/3 cup horseradish
1/3 cup mustard

2/3 cup Worcestershire
sauce
1 1/3 cups lemon or lime
juice (fresh)
3 cups brown sugar
4 teaspoons Tabasco sauce
4 teaspoons celery seed

Melt butter in saucepan. Saute garlic. Add all other ingredients. Simmer over medium-low heat 1/2 to 1 hour. Chill. Use on any barbecue meats. Lasts 6 weeks if covered and refrigerated. Makes 2 quarts.

Diane M. Grady
Philadelphia, PA

Honey-Mustard Chicken

Preparation time: 35 minutes

1 broiler-fryer chicken
(about 2 pounds), halved
2 teaspoons garlic salt
4 tablespoons Dijon
mustard

Juice of 1 lime
1/3 cup honey

Prepare charcoal grill. Sprinkle garlic salt evenly on chicken halves. Place chicken skin side down on a dish or tray. Spread each half with 1/2 tablespoon mustard. Stir lime juice into honey; set aside. Place chicken on grill approximately 6 inches from charcoal for about 15 minutes. Brush lime-honey mixture on chicken and broil an additional 5 minutes. Turn; spread other side with remaining mustard, broil for about 8 minutes or until tender. Baste with remaining lime-honey mixture. Makes 2 servings.

Mary H. Leone
Gilford, Canada

Lamb Shishkebab

Preparation time: 1 hour, 40 minutes

½ cup salad oil
2 tablespoons soy sauce
1 teaspoon Worcestershire sauce
½ teaspoon dry mustard
3 tablespoons lemon juice
1 clove garlic, minced
1 pound leg of lamb, boned and cut in 2-inch cubes

1 green pepper, seeded and cut in 1½-inch strips
12 large size mushrooms
12 cherry tomatoes
12 slices, ½-inch thick, zucchini or eggplant, peeled
6 boiling onions

Combine first 6 ingredients in a bowl and mix well. Add meat cubes, cover and chill about 1 hour. Remove meat from marinade and drain. Thread each of 2 skewers with alternating pieces of meat and vegetables. Place on grill about 6 inches above coals and cook, turning and basting with marinade, until browned and meat slightly pink inside, approximately 20 minutes. Serve on a bed of rice. Makes 2–4 servings.

Rita Egide
Citrus Heights, CA

Limey Caribbean Chicken

Preparation time: 30 minutes

3 *limes*
¼ cup soy sauce
¼ teaspoon rosemary,
  crushed

¼ teaspoon ginger
1 small frying chicken,
  halved or cut-up
  Melted butter (optional)

Juice enough limes to measure ¼ cup. Reserve remaining limes for garnish. Mix lime juice, soy sauce, rosemary and ginger. With sharp knife, slash meaty side of broilers to the bone, at 1-inch intervals. Pour marinade over chicken, in shallow casserole. Marinate 2 hours (or overnight in refrigerator) turning occasionally. Arrange chicken on grill on broiler pan. Brush with melted butter, if desired. Grill frequently with marinade and butter. Serve at once with lime halves. Makes 2 servings.

The working woman can marinate the chicken the night before, come home, and then cook it on an outdoor grill. It tastes its best then.

Kathleen L. Spolarich
Arlington, VA

Marinated Flank Steak

Preparation time: Approximately 15 minutes plus marinating time

½–1 pound flank steak
¼ cup bourbon
¼ cup water
¼ cup oil
¼ cup soy sauce
1 clove garlic, minced

Score flank steak on both sides to allow marinade to penetrate. Combine remaining ingredients. Place steak in dish or plastic marinator or plastic bag. Pour combined liquids and garlic over steak. Marinate at least 8 hours. Broil outside on hot coals or under pre-heated broiler about 5 inches from heat, approximately 5–6 minutes per side for medium rare. Makes 2 servings.

Index